PRACTICAL SOCIAL WORK

Series Editor: Jo Campling

BASW

Editorial Advisory Board:
Robert Adams, Terry Bamford, Charles Barker,
Lena Dominelli, Malcolm Payne, Michael Preston-Shoot,
Daphne Statham and Jane Tunstill

Social work is at an important stage in its development. All professions must be responsive to changing social and economic conditions if they are to meet the needs of those they serve. This series focuses on sound practice and the specific contribution which social workers can make to the well-being of our society.

The British Association of Social Workers has always been conscious of its role in setting guidelines for practice and in seeking to raise professional standards. The conception of the Practical Social Work series arose from a survey of BASW members to discover where they, the practitioners in social work, felt there was the most need for new literature. The response was overwhelming and enthusiastic, and the result is a carefully planned, coherent series of books. The emphasis is firmly on practice set in a theoretical framework. The books will inform, stimulate and promote discussion, thus adding to the further development of skills and high professional standards. All the authors are practitioners and teachers of social work representing a wide variety of experience.

JO CAMPLING

A list of published titles in this series follows overleaf

PRACTICAL SOCIAL WORK

Self-Help, Social Work and Empowerment
Robert Adams

Social Work and Mental Handicap
David Anderson

Beyond Casework
James G. Barber

Citizen Involvement
Peter Beresford and Suzy Croft

Practising Social Work Law
Suzy Braye and Michael Preston-Shoot

Social Workers at Risk
Robert Brown *et al.*

Social Work and Mental Illness
Alan Butler and Colin Pritchard

Social Work and Europe
Crescy Cannan *et al.*

Residential Work
Roger Clough

Social Work and Child Abuse
David M. Cooper and David Ball

Management in Social Work
Veronica Coulshed

Social Work Practice
Veronica Coulshed

Social Work and Local Politics
Paul Daniel and John Wheeler

Sociology in Social Work Practice
Peter R. Day

Anti-Racist Social Work
Lena Dominelli

Working with Abused Children
Celia Doyle

Applied Research for Better Practice
Angela Everitt *et al.*

Student Supervision in Social Work
Kathy Ford and Alan Jones

Working with Rural Communities
David Francis and Paul Henderson

Children, their Families and the Law
Michael D.A. Freeman

Family Work with Elderly People
Alison Froggatt

Child Sexual Abuse
Danya Glaser and Stephen Frosh

Computers in Social Work
Bryan Glastonbury

Working with Families
Gill Gorell Barnes

Women, Management and Care
Cordelia Grimwood and Ruth Popplestone

Women and Social Work
Jalna Hanmer and Daphne Statham

Youth Work
Tony Jeffs and Mark Smith (eds)

Problems of Childhood and Adolescence
Michael Kerfoot and Alan Butler

Communication in Social Work
Joyce Lishman

Social Work with Old People
Mary Marshall

Applied Psychology for Social Workers
Paula Nicolson and Rowan Bayne

Crisis Intervention in Social Services
Kieran O'Hagan

Social Work with Disabled People
Michael Oliver

Care Management
Joan Orme and Bryan Glastonbury

Social Care in the Community
Malcolm Payne

Working in Teams
Malcolm Payne

Working with Young Offenders
John Pitts

Effective Groupwork
Michael Preston-Shoot

Social Work with the Dying and Bereaved
Carole R. Smith

Child Care and the Courts
Carole R. Smith *et al.*

Social Work and Housing
Gill Stewart and John Stewart

Focus on Families
Christine Stones

Anti-Discriminatory Practice
Neil Thompson

Working with Mental Illness
Derek Tilbury

Community Work
Alan Twelvetrees

Working with Offenders
Hilary Walker and Bill Beaumont (eds)

Focus on Families

Family Centres in Action

Christine Stones

Foreword by Roger Singleton

MACMILLAN **M** **Barnardos** in association with BARNARDO'S

First published 1994 by
THE MACMILLAN PRESS LTD
Houndmills, Basingstoke, Hampshire RG21 2XS
and London
Companies and representatives
throughout the world

ISBN 0–333–60232–3 hardcover
ISBN 0–333–60233–1 paperback

A catalogue record for this book is available from the British Library.

Typeset by Florencetype Ltd, Kewstoke, Avon

Printed in Hong Kong

Series Standing Order (Practical Social Work)

If you would like to receive future titles in this series as they are
published, you can make use of our standing order facility. To
place a standing order please contact your bookseller or, in case of
difficulty, write to us at the address below with your name and
address and the name of the series. Please state with which title
you wish to begin your standing order. (If you live outside the UK
we may not have the rights for your area, in which case we will
forward your order to the publisher concerned.)

Standing Order Service, Macmillan Distribution Ltd,
Houndmills, Basingstoke, Hampshire, RG21 2XS, England.

Contents

Foreword by Roger Singleton   viii

Acknowledgements   xi

Introduction   xiii

1 The Family   **1**
A subject for debate   1
Myth and reality   2
The family and its environment   8
The family and the state   11
The family and family centres   17

2 The Evolution of Family Centres   **19**
The precursors of family centres   19
The influence of 'prevention'   20
The move from residential to community care   22
The involvement of parents in early education   23
Other associated factors   24
The Children Act and family centres   24
Literature on family centres   25

3 Models and Philosophies   **29**
The variety of provision   29
Different philosophies   30
Common factors in centres   30
Categorisation of centres   31
Dimensions for identifying differences between centres   33
Creating profiles of family centres   47
An integrated model   49

4 Processes, Services and Resources   **52**
Stages and processes in family centre work   52
Range of activities and services   62
Advice and advocacy   62
Provision of resources   68

5 Approaches and Methods in a Family Centre   **74**
Context and choice of method or approach   74
Working with individuals   76
Working with couples and families   84
Groupwork in a family centre   86
Community work from a family centre base   93

6 A Child Perspective   **102**
The importance of a child perspective   102
Implications of a child perspective   104
Working with individual children   105
Working with groups of children   108
Working with child(ren) and parents together   111
Working with groups of children and parents   114
Paramountcy of the child's welfare   116

7 Partnership with Parents   **117**
Background to partnership   117
Partnership with the individual/family   118
Organisational partnership   120
Defying definition   126
Factors which promote or prevent partnership   128

8 Management Issues (I)   **133**
What is management?   133
Organisational contexts and constraints   135
Power and control   135
Aims and objectives   136
Evaluation   139

9 Management Issues (II)   **144**
Staffing   144
Working with other agencies   153

10 Issues and Challenges for Family Centres **159**
Introduction 159
Who are family centres for? 159
Parents and children together 167
Staff and families together 170
Pointers for wider social welfare provision 174

Bibliography 178

Index 188

Foreword

The past fifteen to twenty years have seen a striking growth in the development of family centres. The approaches pioneered by the centres to meet the needs of children and their carers have their roots in a rich diversity of services and social work methods, including playgroups, nurseries and community work, as well as direct work with families. Their location in the community and the recognition of the interdependency of the needs of adults and children have contributed to the success of family centres and this is particularly reflected in the enthusiasm and support for them shown by users and legislators. The Children Act 1989 has further stimulated this enthusiasm as local authorities, health authorities and the voluntary sector seek to improve ways of meeting the needs of children in all communities.

However, the term 'family centre' can be as misunderstood as the use of the word 'family'. The common perception of families as two parents and two children no longer describes the reality of many families. In reflecting this diversity, family centres offer a range of approaches to meet a variety of purposes in order to tailor their services to the needs of those who use them.

This book is an excursion into the dimensions and critical issues that underlie the generic term 'family centre'. I hope that it will prove useful for students, practitioners, managers and service providers by highlighting common features of family centres and providing some useful frameworks and analyses on which to build.

It is written by staff at Barnardo's Fulford Family Centre in Hartcliffe, Bristol, whose Project Leader, Christine Stones, is the primary author. The centre, which is run by Barnardo's and jointly funded with Avon Social Services Department, opened in 1984. It offers an integrated approach to work with families with children under 5 – providing counselling and therapeutic services, groupwork activities and welfare rights advice, as well as undertaking community development work. From its opening, a central feature has been its emphasis on partnership with parents, and its parents' committees and Parents' Council are established features of the Centre's operation.

At the time of writing all of the original staff group continue to work at the Centre, joined by new team-members. This is a tribute to their capacity to develop and reflect on practice in a way that re-energises and sustains them. Under Christine Stones's leadership the team has developed a range of articles, papers, external research and other studies. They enjoy a mutually beneficial relationship with Professor Phyllida Parsloe and the University of Bristol.

It is on this base of extensive and in-depth experience, coupled with a theoretical and research perspective and wide knowledge of other centres, that the quality and authority of the book rests. It draws together many of the ideas and debates on family centres and develops understanding of the processes and issues at the heart of family centre work. Christine Stones identifies the different dimensions of centres in her typology outlined in Chapter 3. The attention to issues of partnership with parents, gender and race is a recurrent theme of the book. Practical examples give depth and illumination to the discussion of more abstract issues. It is a readable, informative and thought-provoking book.

Barnardo's takes no special credit for the development of the family centre approach. A wide variety of individuals and organisations, both voluntary and statutory, have contributed to the innovative work which is characteristic of centres nationwide. Similarly, Fulford Family Centre does not claim to have all the answers. It does, however, face all the dilemmas which readers with knowledge and experience of family centre work will recognise. I join the contributors to this book in hoping that everyone involved with family centres will find it of value in the continuing development of effective and non-discriminating services which meet the needs of children, families and the wider community.

ROGER SINGLETON
Senior Director
Barnardo's

Acknowledgements

This book is attributed to a single author but several people were responsible. The stimulus for publishing arose from the experiences of a group of staff initiating and developing one family centre. Writing the book has been a team effort and would have been impossible without the team's commitment and enthusiasm.

Individual written contributions were as follows:

Frances Fox	counselling
Owen Gill	evaluation
Phil Holford	welfare rights and organisational partnership with parents
Terry Jones	groupwork
Maggie Proom	community work
Jackie Sims	community work and practical and material resources
Dave Smith	management issues I
Penny Snow	volunteers

In addition, Felicity Marks and Jackie Sims were central in producing the ideas for the Child Perspective chapter.

We are grateful to Jane Crane for obtaining feedback from Fulford parents and greatly appreciated the willingness of so many parents to share their experiences of Fulford with Jane.

Owen Gill, Daphne Norbury, Phyllida Parsloe, Drew Reith, Jill Reynolds and Dave Smith provided helpful comments on the draft manuscript. I am particularly indebted also to Daphne Norbury for her willing assistance with the detail and intelligibility of the final text. Sue Gaines's support was vital in ensuring that Fulford's administration continued smoothly over months of my preoccupation with writing and editing. All of the above-named also provided the encouragement necessary for the completion of this book.

As a staff team we are indebted to Barnardo's, in particular our Divisional Management Team and Nora Dixon (Coordinator for Research and Development), for making time available for us to write. The resources of the Barnardo's library staff, David Potter, Frank Emmott and Joan Pickton, were invaluable.

The interest and support of family and friends, throughout the long process of writing and editing, has been essential.

Lastly, but above all, we are grateful to all the families who have shared so freely and enabled us to learn so much as together we have discovered the role of family centres.

CHRISTINE STONES

Introduction

The inspiration for this book arose from the experience gained by a team of workers in establishing Fulford Family Centre, a Barnardo's project, in Bristol. The centre opened in 1984 and since then the staff have learned an enormous amount from each other and from the families using the centre. Fulford Family Centre, like the majority of such centres, works with young children and thus issues relevant to work with families with young children are a major focus of this book. The centre is neighbourhood-based and has developed an integrated approach to work with families. This is founded on a philosophy which views the problems and possibilities facing families with young children as arising from a number of interacting factors. Such a perspective refuses to locate issues of child development, neglect or abuse either solely within the individual family or simply within the community or social structures. Rather it recognises the multiple, interconnected factors which must be addressed when considering the health and development of children and their families.

The staff and centre have also gained much from contact with workers and participants in other centres through the Family Centre Network and other channels. Therefore, although the book arose from immersion in one particular family centre, it is informed by theory-and-practice wisdom from numerous other sources. As will be seen, family centres are so multifarious that it is impossible to provide one comprehensive text which is utterly relevant to them all. However, family centres have enough in common for it to be hoped that anyone with an interest in them will discover valuable material in this text.

Whilst diverse sources have contributed to this book, inevitably the greatest influences have been the experience of a specific staff group in a particular family centre. As a result certain important perspectives are either absent or 'borrowed' and some issues are not covered comprehensively. This is perhaps most obvious in terms of race and disability. The authors and the largest majority of the families participating in Fulford Family Centre are white and able-bodied and this will probably be very apparent. Nevertheless, anti-discriminatory practice should underpin the work of every family centre regardless of the composition of staff group or families served. So in this book, as in our work, we have attempted to grapple with the implications of oppression and discrimination and have sought to make the family centre equally accessible to and effective for all families. In some instances it has been difficult to find sources of published material which compensate for limitations of experience and provide broader perspectives.

The concerns of any family centre are so extensive and varied that a rich expanse of literature bears some relevance to its work. As a result, an introductory text to family centres has to be highly selective. Several large textbooks have been written on areas which this book mentions in a passing paragraph. Hence, for example, little or no detail is provided about fundamental principles of child protection, family therapy or practice teaching but a variety of excellent sources already exist on these and other pertinent subjects. This may at times be frustrating for readers, but the intention is to cover those aspects most important to family centres on the assumption that readers will consult other texts for more detailed theory and practice.

In attempting to produce a coherent account of family centres and their work, a certain structure and order has been imposed. Readers familiar with life in a family centre may find that this presents them with an air of unreality at times! It is difficult to capture in the written word the liveliness and flux, the heights and depths of experiences, the seeming chaos and confusion, the delights and demands which are the reality of most family centres.

1

The Family

A subject for debate

The family is the subject of much debate. It has both attackers and defenders. The desirability and viability of its existence is argued. Answers to many and varied fundamental questions are pursued. Is the family biologically determined or socially constructed? Should the family be a private haven or a focus of public concern? Is the family a universal and enduring institution or a feature of particular social orders? Are there advantages of specific structures or patterns of family life?

As families are the focus of family centres, it is apposite that an exploration of family centres begins with a brief enquiry into some of the issues surrounding 'the family'. A simple, unambiguous and useful definition of the family is surprisingly difficult to achieve. Morgan (1985) tackles the problem at the end of his enquiry into the family. He suggests that we understand that:

> the word 'family' has something to do with marriage and parenthood and that these two terms themselves have something to do with, respectively, the relationships between adults and the relationships between adults and children, these two sets of relationships being focused on something that may be called a home or a household (Morgan, 1985, p. 269)

Brief consideration of the above statement rapidly reveals the inherent problems in understanding what is meant by 'the family'. Marriage can be understood in varied ways: it may be limited to a legal or religious status or encompass cohabitation. Also for many families the word 'family' incorporates relationships which are not confined to one household.

Rapoport and Rapoport (1982, p. 475) provide a somewhat broader statement when they write, 'Families – intimate domestic groups made up of people related to one another by bonds of blood, sexual mating or legal tie – have been our most durable social unit.'

There is agreement that in the past century the family has been influenced by several and varied factors. These have included reliable contraception, labour-saving household devices, a general rise in the standard of living (from which some have benefited more than others), a marked reduction in infant mortality, extended life-expectancy, increasing divorce and remarriage rates, migration and geographical mobility.

Myth and reality

To speak or write of *the* family invokes multifarious assumptions and myths. It is an institution which exerts a powerful influence on the lives of each individual and as such makes objective study a difficult task. Thus we all bring to any consideration of families and family life, our own enriching and damaging family experiences. Our beliefs and prejudices about the structure, patterns and nature of family life are formulated both by our individual life histories and by the images we absorb from around us.

It is therefore essential that anyone engaged in work with families and thus anyone concerned with family centres should be aware of the prevailing individual and communal myths. Without an examination of assumptions and conceptions, there is a serious danger of reaching a false conclusion of shared understandings. Work in a family centre requires an openness to the unique reality of each family and its members. Whilst there will be individual susceptibility to particular fables and fantasies, a number of popular myths and the contrasting reality can be explored.

Family structure and its effects on family members

There is increasing recognition of the changes that have taken place in household structures and family composition and the resultant variety of family settings. However there is still a tendency for 'the family' to be represented by images of two biological parents and their two children or for only limited variations to be recognised. Thus the *General Household Survey*, for example, defines the family as 'a married couple living alone or with their children, or a lone parent with his or her children, in each case the children being never married'. 'Their' children in any definition is fraught with confusion as the variety of possible relationships between children and the adults in 'their' family of residence is considerable. There are biological parents, step-parents, foster parents, adoptive parents and so on. In one household there may be any combination of such relationships between children and adults. During their childhood, many children will experience more than one family structure.

There are different family structures existing within varied minority ethnic groups. The 'traditional' structure in any society has emerged through particular cultural and religious influences and there is always a danger of white workers viewing family structures from a 'Eurocentric' norm.

A fact sheet from the Family Policy Studies Centre states:

> The growing diversity of family patterns has received widespread public and political attention in recent years. Nevertheless, continuities in family life are also important. It remains the case today that most people in Britain marry and have children and that most marriages last a lifetime (Fact Sheet 1, *The Family Today*, 1991).

Thus there is the continuity of what has been termed a 'traditional' family model alongside a number of different family models. There can be a danger of viewing this 'traditional' model as somehow superior or of greater benefit to its members, and specifically to children, than other models. A considerable amount of research has been conducted on the functioning of a variety of family structures. This research has studied lone-parent families, social-contract families, families in communes and lesbian households. The findings suggest that children can develop healthy personalities in a wide variety of family structures (Schaffer,1988).

Attention has been drawn to the impact of prejudice and stereotyping on children living in 'non-traditional' families. This is demonstrated by a study by Fry and Addington (1984) which revealed that the judgement of both lay persons and professionals about a child's development were markedly influenced by negative expectations of the impact of particular family types.

Research suggests that it is the quality of family relationships which is a key influence on a child's development, rather than any specific family structure. Schaffer (1988) points out:

> Ongoing discord has considerably worse consequences for children than even a complete break in the relationship with a parent. This emerges from comparisons of children who have lost a parent through death with children who have lost the parent through divorce. It is also seen when one compares children whose parents conducted their separation in a reasonably amicable fashion with those where divorce was part of a long drawn-out saga of conflict.

Family patterns

Family centre workers need to recognise that there is considerable diversity in the patterns of roles and relationships within families. This reality contrasts with a 'popular' image of the family. The family of 'traditional' structure was frequently viewed as functioning according to 'conventional' roles and relationships; the stereotype being the breadwinning father and the housekeeping, child-rearing mother. Frequently authority in the family would be based on a patriarchal model. Parsons (1970) attached roles to gender suggesting that the expressive role in the family is always played by the woman and the instrumental role by the man – the latter being seen as the dominant role. This both stereotyped the sex roles and falsely assumed that such roles are mutually exclusive.

Patterns of family life are influenced by differences in class, culture, beliefs, and values. As Rapoport and Rapoport (1982) point out when considering the impact of cultural differences:

> These differences affect not only gender-role conceptions and internal family division of labour and child-rearing, but also attitudes to work, education, social institutions and other elements in the social environment (Rapoport and Rapoport, 1982, p. 480)

In Britain minority ethnic groups offer a rich plurality of family organisation. Ballard (1982) outlines the common factors and some of the differences in family patterns within communities of South Asian origin. Driver (1982) and Barrow (1982) provide perspectives on West Indian families. Bryan (1992) explores some of the myths and reality of Afro-Caribbean families. Asian women's powerful accounts of their experiences of family life are documented by Wilson (1978). Oakley (1979) describes Cypriot patterns of family, kinship and patronage. Goody and Groothues (1979) identify differences between Ashanti and Ibo culture in West African families in Britain. However, as Dominelli (1988) points out, recognition and appreciation of the rich diversity of black family patterns is rare. Yet as the authors of *Race in Child Protection* emphasise:

> One culture can learn much from another about childhood, parenting, education and family life. Diversity of culture is enriching and different cultural and ethnic values and family forms are sources of strength (Race Equality Unit, 1990, p. 2).

Differences exist not only between ethnic groups but across the total population. In British society there is an enormous variety of family arrangements. There are families where one or both parent(s) work and families where neither parent is employed. There are lone parents in employment and unemployed lone parents. In some families child care is shared between parents and in others either the mother or the father is the primary carer. There continue to be patriarchal families but there are also matriarchal families and families where authority is shared. There is heterogeneity in the role and influence of the extended family.

Many writers point out that although a number of changes have taken place in family life and a diversity of patterns exist, child care and domestic tasks continue to rest mainly with mothers (Allan, 1985; Hanmer and Statham, 1988; Leonard and Speakman, 1986). The different usage of the verbs 'to mother' and 'to father' indicate society's divergent expect-ations of involvement with children. 'To father' is to promote or produce something whilst 'to mother' involves cherishing or looking after. Despite a major increase in the employment of women the extent to which home tasks are shared appears limited. As Langan (1992) writes:

> Numerous surveys have confirmed that the complementary emergence of the 'new man' who takes his fair share in domestic and child care tasks remains a fiction (Langan, 1992, p. 69).

There is also evidence that points to unemployment having little impact on the traditional role divisions within families. Allan (1985, p. 162) suggests that, 'unemployment may well encourage a polarization of male and female activities rather than any convergence between them'. One of the factors he identifies as contributing to the lack of convergence is the fact that gender identities are created through many years of socialisation.

The influence of different family patterns on children is debated but no research evidence appears to demonstrate that children fare better within one family pattern rather than another:

> Many alternative social arrangements are developmentally sound; they are different but equal. Therefore, we are led to a commitment to pluralism, to letting families utilize and pursue their different strategies and tactics for producing competent children within some common agreement on basic principles such as the need for love, affection and acceptance (Garbarino, 1982, p. 2).

Needs and experiences within the family

In Western societies, the family is the institution which provides for the majority of physical, developmental and emotional needs of children. Children who are cared for in settings other than a family are usually regarded as disadvantaged. The family is also the focus for the identity, aspirations and emotional needs of many adults.

A myth which requires exploration is the misleading notion of *family* needs and experiences. As Leonard and Speakman (1986, p. 8) point out 'there is a tension between the idea that the family is a unit with shared aims and interests and the fact that the individual members of a family often have conflicting needs and desires'. The needs of individuals within families are sometimes in mutual harmony and sometimes competing. This is most readily apparent in the satisfactions and frustrations experienced between partners and between parents and children.

Because of structural factors such as race, gender, class and age, individual family members have very different experiences within the same family (Thorne and Yalom *et al.*, 1982; A. Hudson, 1989). As indicated in the preceding section, women tend to carry the major responsibility for child care and domestic life. Yet motherhood is an ambiguous role:

> Motherhood is often seen as leisure rather than work. Looking after children is acknowledged neither as hard work, nor as worthwhile (Calvert, 1985, p. 57).

> Motherhood is both idealised and denigrated (Pugh and De'Ath, 1984, p. 207).

The studies of Brown and Harris (1978) demonstrated that being at home full time with small children without paid employment increases a woman's vulnerability to depression.

For some women the family is an arena of inequality, domination and violence inflicted by their male partners. Children may experience similar disadvantage and abuse through the adult members of their households. A family may treat boys very differently from girls. Thus some boys grow up enjoying greater freedom and opportunities than their sisters, whilst girls may be offered greater possibilities of emotional development. Eichenbaum and Orbach (1985) explore how the different experiences of boys and girls in infancy and childhood shape their psychological development as men and women.

Differences exist not only between the fortunes of husband and wife, parent and child, and brother and sister but also men, women and children in different families will have contrasting experiences as wives and mothers, husbands and fathers, sons and brothers, and daughters and sisters. The wider context will influence an individual's perspective on family experience. Thus white women in a white male-dominated society may experience the family as confirming and reinforcing oppression whilst, as Dominelli (1988) and Hanmer and Statham (1988) indicate, black women may find the family a vital source of strength and encouragement in a racist society:

> The family is an important means by which black women and men, children and young people, can gain a positive image of themselves and avoid the powerlessness that comes from the negative valuation placed on them by external sources (Hanmer and Statham, 1988, p. 14).

Families for many individuals are the source of both pain and joy, Wilson (1978) quotes the poignant words of an Asian woman:

> My family is like a part of myself, of my body; if I cut it off I could die. But it is a part which gives me so much pain that sometimes I can't bear it – can't bear it at all.

The family and its environment

The family can be viewed as standing at the interface between the individual and society. Socialisation is primarily fulfilled within the family. Every family member is situated in a complex network of relationships between individual, family and social environment. One conceptual framework which helps in any analysis and understanding of this seeming labyrinth is general systems theory. This has been applied and developed as an ecological approach to children and families by writers such as Bronfenbrenner (1979) and Garbarino (1982).

This formulation, drawing on insights from many disciplines, examines both the contexts of the individual, such as family, school, neighbourhood and the interconnectedness of these different systems. An ecological framework assumes that the individual acts on his/her environment and vice versa. Such a framework recognises the power of factors beyond individuals and their families to enhance or impoverish their lives and thus apprehends the impact of social structures and of public and communal organisation on the family. So, for example, the injustices and inequalities suffered by black children and their families through racism can be identified as a most profound influence on their quality of life.

Individual children's and families' lives are affected by a myriad of interacting components. An indication of the number and range is provided by the following list, which is not exhaustive:

● the child's innate physical and intellectual predispositions;
● the parent(s)' or other primary care-givers' physical and emotional resources;
● the character of relationships within the family and with friends, neighbours and wider kin;
● the nature of relationships with formal networks, such as health, education, or social services;
● the immediate physical and material circumstances, including food, clothing, warmth and shelter;
● the wider physical setting such as housing and road design, shopping and recreational facilities;
● the nature, demands or absence of parental employment;
● public and private policies and provision relating to a vast range of issues such as employment, health, education, housing, transportation, maternity and paternity leave, pre-school and after-school care;

● the extent of personal and institutional racism;
● social attitudes, norms and values for example relating to family violence, racism and sexism.

Opportunities and risks for children and their families

Using an ecological perspective Garbarino (1982) introduces the notion of sociocultural risks and opportunities. This highlights the fact that each of the systems interacting with a child has the potential for being a positive or a negative influence. Hence different families are faced with varied opportunities and risks and these relate to the factors listed above.

The multiplicity and interaction of the factors which create benefits and problems for children and their families must be borne in mind. Otherwise there is a tendency to polarise causation which either relates advantage and disadvantage solely to factors within the individual and their family or simply to social structures. The reality, as an ecological perspective emphasises, is a complex synthesis. Applying this, for example, to parenting as Quinton and Rutter (1988) infer:

> parenting is a multifactorial function that is reliant on a range of personal, material and social resources. These include the time available; the person's own emotional state; the presence of other life stresses and problems; the qualities of the spouse; the extent to which child-rearing is shared; the existence of other satisfactions and achievements apart from parenting (as in a job outside the home): the availability of adequate social supports and housing conditions.

Gill's (1992) research provides vivid illustrations of the interrelated pressures which face parents caring for children in disadvantaged areas.

Family centres will frequently be in contact with families where risks are more apparent than opportunities. The children and their families, portrayed below will seem familiar to most family centres:

> Daniel, born with a disability, is faced with greater risks and fewer opportunities than a child without disability. The difficul-

ties for Daniel, and his family, are compounded by the family's poverty, lack of private transport, accommodation in a multi-storey flat with unreliable lifts and at some distance from supportive family and friends.

Jenny's parenting behaviour is influenced by abuse in her own childhood, the hyperactivity of her child, the absence of a partner, her one-bedroomed flat and limited material resources and social supports.

Maria is unhappy at school, the size of which confuses her. She is the only black child in her class and is the subject of racist abuse. She has not revealed her school experiences at home as she fears it will add to her mother's anxiety and depression.

Sarah and James rarely play outside. They live in a low-rise block of flats with no fenced garden. The green outside the flats is frequented by drug-users and discarded needles are often discovered. They live in an area of high unemployment and neither of their parents has been able to obtain employment.

One of the features of modern society is the extent of the media and of advertising. Both present a whole range of family images and 'stories'. The degree to which they are sources of opportunity or risk is difficult to evaluate and little if any research exists to aid such an assessment. It is clear that they may enlarge understandings of family structures and patterns or they may foster stereotypes and prejudice. They may encourage imagination and widen horizons or they may pressurise and discourage as they present unattainable visions and dreams.

The family and the state

One of the macrosystems most influential for family life is the state. As Land and Parker (1978) (p. 331) point out 'Britain has never had an integrated set of social policies explicitly termed "family policies".' Yet most economic and social policies have wide-ranging effects on family life and their direction arises from particular ideological positions. Thus taxation clauses and social security regulations have underlying assumptions as to the dependence or independence of husbands and wives and the responsibility for children.

Certain household patterns may be encouraged by social policies whilst others may be undermined:

> social policies reinforce and sometimes privilege household units characterized by female dependency and a particular sexual division of labour. But other assumptions underpin the policies and practices around families – namely, heterosexual coupledom, race, ethnicity and able-bodiedness – in ways that penalize and pathologize (Williams, 1992, p. 18).

There are competing ideologies concerning the relationship between the state and the family. Fox Harding (1991) identifies four different value perspectives which can underlie the role taken by the state in relation to children and families. These are (i) a *'laissez-faire* and patriarchy' position which encourages a minimal role for the state, (ii) a 'state paternalism and child protection' perspective which legitimises active intervention by the state. The maintenance of children in their birth families is supported by (iii) a 'modern defence of the birth family and parents' rights' perspective. View (iv), 'children's rights and child liberation', seeks to emphasise the child as an independent person with his/her own viewpoint and wishes. The four perspectives give differing weight to children's rights, parents' rights and the right of the state to intervene in family life.

Other ideologies focus on responsibilities rather than rights. The New Right's approach, assumes that the family has primary, if not sole, responsibility for child-rearing and for caring for any dependent members and the state's role is only to intervene where families fail in their responsibilities. From this perspective, policies of community care usually mean family care and in the vast majority of instances this equates to care being provided by women. A contrasting philosophy views family issues from a collective rather than an individualist position and urges state responsibility for dependent members of society. Coussins and Coote (1981) express this view:

Family policy should recognise that children are our most precious resource and that everyone has an obligation to them, whether parents or not.

Legislation and families

As Turner (1986) points out:

> legal images of the family simultaneously constitute a model of and a model for socially acceptable family behaviour. Such models tend to be conservative. They serve as practical guides to prescribed, permitted and prohibited behaviour (Turner, 1986, p. 25).

The family and its members have been the subject both directly and indirectly of much legislation over the years. Every statute expresses particular values and norms. Some child care legislation appears to have been motivated by 'child rescue' and other by 'parental rights'. Bainham (1990) indicates that the Children Act 1989 brings about essential reforms which will require the State to pay proper regard to the fundamental human rights of parents and children as required by the European Convention on Human Rights.

The Act is a notable development which appears to synthesise certain features of each of the value positions defined by Fox Harding (1991) and denoted above. As the Guidance and Regulations associated with the Act states:

> The Children Act 1989 brings together in a single coherent legislative framework the private and public law relating to children. It aims to strike a balance between the rights of children to express their views on decisions made about their lives, the rights of parents to exercise their responsibilities towards the child and the duty of the state to intervene where the child's welfare requires it (Department of Health, 1991).

One of the principles of the Act is 'non-intervention' by the courts which suggests a *'laissez-faire'* perspective. At the same time the Act was clearly influenced by a number of child-abuse enquiries and thus a key theme is the effective protection of children by the state. The Act also demonstrates values associated with 'the modern defence of the family and parents' rights' view as 'An Introduction to the Children Act' shows:

> The Act rests on the belief that children are generally best looked after within the family with both parents playing a full part without resort to legal proceedings (Department of Health, 1989).

Some hints of a 'children's rights and child liberation' position are detected in the emphasis in the Act on the paramountcy of the child's welfare and the requirement to attend to the child's wishes.

Responsibilities are central to the Act's philosophy and one of its radical themes is the idea of parental responsibility rather than parental rights. But it also encourages partnership between parents and local authorities, the latter having duties to aid parents in the care of their children. As Packman and Jordan (1991) point out:

> So, in the Act parenting is for life, because children need continuity, security and a sense of identity. But it also asserts that parents may need assistance in exercising their responsibilities.
> . . .

Two other features of the Children Act also need highlighting and their implications are explored by Macdonald (1991). First, the Act places emphasis on a child's race, culture, religion and language. Due consideration must be given to these factors both when a local authority is looking after a child (section 22[5][c]) and in making arrangements for provision of day care (schedule 2). This requires practitioners and managers to pay rigorous attention to what is really in the interest and for the welfare of black children and their families. As Ahmad (1990, p. 89) urges:

> all sections of the Children Act have implications for Black Children, not just the specific sections referring to race, religion and ethnic origin. It must then follow that if social workers are to fulfil all their promoting and protecting duties, then their practice with Black children has to be non-racist and non-discriminatory.

Such practice requires that workers really listen to and involve black children, parents and communities.

Second, the Children Act 1989 (together with the National Health Service and Community Care Act 1990) has important implications for children with a disability and for their families. As Begum (1991) states, 'The Children Act heralds a major advance in recognising the needs, wishes and aspirations of children with disabilities as children in their own right.'

Many commentators question whether the resources are being made available to make local authority support to families the reality the Act proposes. As Begum (1991) argues:

> The Children Act and the Community Care Act could provide the keystones for a range of effective, efficient, and sensitive services. But without a political, practical and financial commitment, particularly in terms of the black and ethnic minority communities, it will continue to be like so much that has gone before – a vessel of empty promises – not worth the paper it is published on.

The Children Act requires local authorities to provide family centres as one of the range of support services to families.

The family and welfare services

The nature and extent of welfare services at any time will relate to the prevailing ideologies held by the state and, to some degree, those of the welfare professions. The objectives underlying welfare provision are varied and may be conflicting. Public services for families are sometimes clearly dependent on the needs of the state. The familiar example of this fact is the expansion in public pre-school day-care in wartime when women were needed in the munitions factories. Provision rapidly decreased when women were no longer essential to the labour market.

A central dilemma for services is the question of universal or selective provision. The welfare state contains a complex mixture of both types of benefits and services. For example, Child Benefit is a benefit payable for all children but many benefits in kind, such as day care, are not available to all children. The 1989 Children Act defines certain responsibilities of the local authority to provide services for children and their families. The issue of selectivity is tackled by introducing the concept of 'children in need'. The Act defines a child as 'in need' if:

(a) he is unlikely to achieve or maintain, or to have the opportunity of achieving or maintaining, a reasonable standard of health or development without the provision for him of services by a local authority under this Part;
(b) his health or development is likely to be significantly impaired, or further impaired, without the provision for him of such services;
  or
(c) he is disabled.

As writers such as Frost (1992) point out, the definition is fraught with difficulties and has certain disadvantages for children and their families. Whilst resource constraints may be used to justify some targeting of services, targeting may well exclude children needing provision and also stigmatises those in receipt of services. The Children Act does not address the support and resources which all families need in order to provide adequate care for children (David, 1991).

There are some emphases in the Children Act which suggest a wider preventive approach to services for families. However this is not congruent with most of the social policy concurrent with the 1989 Act and the associated restraints on local government expenditure. Many commentators have pointed to 'a new era' in welfare provision in Britain. Langan (1992, p. 67) highlights two themes apparent in the transformation of the personal social services. First, 'the promotion of the family as a key agency of care and control in society' and second the move from the local authority as provider of services to the role of an enabler.

The relationship between the family and welfare services is most usually centred on the mother. As Balbo (1987, p. 49) points out:

It is women who keep in touch with teachers and school staff, who take children to clinics and hospitals, who visit welfare agencies to obtain the family's entitlement.'

Factors contributing to these gendered arrangements include the social construction of the mother as responsible for servicing the family's needs and the access to much welfare provision being limited to 'working hours'.

Hallett (1989) points out some of the contradictions in welfare provision when she writes of social services departments:

> They have a potential to provide valued and needed services to women and others, who are often vulnerable and disadvantaged, but they may do so on terms which are paternalistic, repressive and which have at their core sexist and racist assumptions about women, social care and domestic life (Hallett, 1989, p. 43).

The family and family centres

As this chapter indicates there are a whole range of issues connected with the family and its position as mediator between the individual and society. Family centres are firmly embedded in the values and history of child-care provision and are inevitably enmeshed in these issues.

There are varying opinions as to the ideologies underlying the establishment of family centres. For example, David (1985) suggests they may be preventive measures supported by New Right and other 'pro-family' groups to reverse demographic and economic trends in patterns of family life. Cannan (1986) warns that, 'family centres may be seen as a way of accomplishing the transfer of welfare service from the state back into the family, and stressing the responsibility of the mother for care and socialisation'. Holman (1988) and other writers describe the potential of family centres for empowerment of family members. Cigno (1988) describes how the services of a family centre, 'enables adults and children to increase their skills, confidence and self-esteem'.

Family centres face a range of questions and dilemmas and some of the more central ones are outlined below:

Are family centres evidence of public concern to assist parents in the care of children or are they agents mainly emphasising parental responsibility for children?

Are family centres solely for families whom professionals, on behalf of the state, identify as failing in fulfilling parental responsibilities or is their purpose to support any family in its arduous tasks?

Do family centres actively seek to engage fathers or do they perpetuate assumptions that child care is 'women's work'?

Do centres provide activities for adults, recognising the needs of individual family members or are they addressing adults solely as parents?

Do family centres mainly address difficulties within individuals and families and ignore the wider systems which prevail upon them?

Do family centres require or assume certain family structures or patterns, for example are their services based on 'Eurocentric' values and perceptions?

These and other questions will be addressed as we explore the nature and development of family centres.

2

The Evolution of Family Centres

The precursors of family centres

Family Centres began to emerge in Britain in the 1970s and a number of factors appear to have been influential in their evolution. Some provision with a much longer history and other facilities which have disappeared seem to share significant features with the centres that have been established in the final decades of the twentieth century.

There have been forerunners of family centres in both the statutory and voluntary sectors. Amongst voluntary agencies Family Service Units in major cities have a long and impressive history of working with disadvantaged families and communities. For a considerable length of time these units were the only agencies concentrating on whole families. Anyone familiar with University Settlements will recognise some aspects in common with family centres.

In the work of local authorities, family centres have not been without predecessors although current centres have evolved from a number of sources. During the 1960s, in response to the Children and Young Persons Act of 1963, several local authorities established Family Advice Services. As Leissner (1967) pointed out, the concepts underlying these centres were early prevention and regarding the family as the basic client unit. There was no single model for these centres; some were units within the local authority Children's Department, others existed in partnership with a voluntary agency and yet others were separate centres serving specific neighbourhoods and communities. Younghusband (1978)

19

refers to the affinity of family advice centres with settlements:

> Then came a period during the 1960s when family advice centres
> . . . and other experiments were discovering independently what
> settlements had pioneered . . .

The eventual fate of family advice centres is unclear and undocumented. It seems probable that they were overtaken by the Seebohm Report and the subsequent remit of Social Services Departments to provide a unified family service.

The influence of 'prevention'

Prevention in child care is frequently associated with the Children and Young Persons Act of 1963. However as Parker (1990, p. 98) points out:

> The legislation of 1963 is . . . a rather misleading landmark in the
> history of prevention in child care, not least because the principle
> of prevention . . . had been invoked from the earliest days of
> organised child care.

The earliest focus for prevention had been prevention of harm to children, the most frequent source of harm being defined as neglectful or violent parents. Thus prevention was fulfilled by 'rescuing' children from their damaging homes. However, a much wider principle of prevention is apparent from the Home Office circular (8 July 1948) which was issued to Local Authorities on the passing of the Children Act that year. It stated:

> Where a home can be so improved that it is unnecessary to
> remove the child from his parents or that a child who has been
> taken away for a time can be properly restored to his parents'
> care, the advantages of this course is unquestionable . . . To keep
> the family together must be the first aim . . .

Prevention is used loosely and therefore often confusingly.

Parker (1980) clarifies our thinking about prevention by utilising the medical classification of three levels of prevention:

- Primary prevention is viewed as relating to those services which 'provide general support to families and reduce the levels of poverty, stress, insecurity, ill-health or bad housing to which they may otherwise be exposed.'
- Secondary prevention focuses on services to families who have been identified as being at particular risk in some way. Services may be designed to alleviate the problem or at least prevent further deterioration of circumstances.
- Tertiary prevention seeks to avoid a problem recurring and to seek the most appropriate solution. Thus tertiary prevention may also be viewed as remedial action.

The three levels of prevention in relation to child abuse can be illustrated as:

> delivering treatment to a parent who has abused a child is remedial, or tertiary prevention. Identifying families at risk of abuse and offering them services to reduce this risk is secondary prevention. Promoting nonviolent and emotionally supportive child rearing is considered primary prevention for child abuse (Garbarino, 1982, pp. 180–1).

The secondary level of prevention, whilst recognised as a principle from the earliest days of public child care, gained particular momentum during the 1960s. The establishment of Family Advice Centres referred to above appears to be the result of this impetus which followed the Ingleby Report (1960) and the subsequent Children and Young Persons Act.

The emergence of Family Centres since the 1970s would appear to be associated with a further emphasis on prevention. Pringle (1982, p. 13) sees community-based family centres in these terms – 'The emphasis would be on normality and prevention rather than on crisis intervention, disease or treatment.' Parker (1990) commenting on the extent to which local authorities are assisting children within their families, identifies a number of factors which have encouraged a preventive perspective against considerable impeding forces. Three such factors he suggests are:

1. the growing recognition of the damage done to children by separation;
2. alarm at the escalation in the number of children in care in the 1970s;
3. the belief that prevention (like restoration) would help to reduce expenditure (Parker, 1990, p. 101).

These would appear to have been important influences in the development of family centres.

The move from residential to community care

The success of policies to reduce the number of children in local authority care is reflected to some degree in the large-scale closures of children's homes by both local authorities and voluntary child care organisations, although clearly an equally important reason for these closures has been a recognition that, in most instances, family placement rather than institutional care is more appropriate to the needs of children. There has also been an economic factor in the closure of much residential provision – family placement being cheaper.

Whilst many homes were closed, others were involved in major changes in philosophy and practice as they moved from providing a substitute home to becoming part of a process to secure help for children within the context of their own or substitute families.

In some local authorities the closures of children's homes allowed a considerable transfer of resources from caring for children separated from their families to attempting to prevent unnecessary separation. Several family centres have evolved from this development. The relationship between the residential establishment and the family centre is sometimes direct and obvious and in other contexts indirect and hardly apparent. The connection between the family centre and the predecessor home can be so close that the change sometimes appears little more than a renaming exercise with some developments in practice. For example, the establishment still provides residential places for children but puts more emphasis on working with families towards rehabilitation. There is a direct but less close connection in other instances where a children's home has been closed, the building redesigned and the staff posts redesignated to establish a family centre. In other cases the family centre has been a more indirect result of the closure, with the funding being released to set up a new project with no other linkage with the closed provision.

The involvement of parents in early education

One of the landmarks of parental involvement in education is the Plowden Report (Department of Education and Science, 1967). This is apparent from its statement: 'It has long been recognised that education is concerned with the whole man: henceforth it must be concerned with the whole family.' Most subsequent education reports have stressed the importance of close relationships between home and school and thus there has been some notion of parental participation. The Taylor Report (Department of Education and Science, 1977) led to the appointment of parent-governors.

This movement within education was paralleled by similar influences in provision of day care for preschool children. Increasingly staff were encouraged to work with parents as well as with children. A joint DHSS/DES circular 'Co-ordination of Services for the Under-Fives' argued:

> services for preschool children must be seen in the context of support for the family as a whole. They should complement and supplement but not serve as a substitute for parental care. Parents' knowledge of and concern for, the needs of their own children needs building on, not replacing.

Thus policies of parental involvement were developed in preschool services. In some settings this was not only an aim for staff but a requirement on parents – for example, places were sometimes offered to the child(ren) with the proviso that the parent also attended for a proportion of the time.

The considerable growth in the preschool playgroup movement, led by parents, was a further factor pressing for parental participation in provision. But as Ferri and Saunders (1991, p. 8) point out, 'there are significant differences in the circumstances leading to parental involvement with various preschool services'. Whilst educational provision and the playgroup movement emphasise the contribution of parents to a child's development, day care as selective social-welfare provision tends to focus on parents as the 'problem' leading to the necessity of day care.

Whilst day care, education and the preschool playgroup movement all emphasise parental involvement, it needs to be acknowledged that it is usually mothers who are the participants.

Other associated factors

There are a number of other factors which appear to have affected the development of family centres although their influence appears less direct. Thus a concern to work with the whole family was given impetus by a growing interest in family therapy within the field of psychiatry and subsequently social work.

The 'cycle of deprivation' propounded by a series of speeches by Sir Keith Joseph in 1972 and 1973 led to recommendations of work with parents and playgroups for children (Fuller and Stevenson, 1983).

A further influence has been a trend towards neighbourhood-based work or community social work as encouraged by the Barclay Report (1982).

The Children Act and family centres

Packman and Jordan (1991) comment on the Children Act 1989 taking 'a quantum leap from the old, restricted notions of "prevention", to a more positive outreaching duty of "support to children and families" '. The Children Act gives Local Authorities a general duty 'to provide such family centres as they consider appropriate in relation to children in their area'. Such provision is part of the family support services which will fulfil a local authority's duty under the Act to promote the upbringing of children by their families.

This is likely to be influential in the development of family centres and will no doubt have impact on the type of centres into which resources will be invested. The Act defines family centres as:

> places where a child, his parents and anyone who has parental responsibility for or is looking after him may go for occupational, social, cultural or recreational activities or advice, guidance or counselling or the person may be accommodated whilst he is receiving advice, guidance or counselling.

The Department of Health Guidance and Regulations indicate that the general duty to provide family centres is not confined to children in need. They also point out that provision can be made directly by the local authority or the local authority can facilitate the provision by voluntary agencies. Good practice, represented in the principles of the Children Act, requires family centres to ensure that their provision is truly accessible to families of varied ethnicity and to children and families with a disability.

Literature on family centres

Literature on family centres is not extensive. There are a number of articles in journals and published papers which describe and in some instances evaluate the work of individual centres. These include Cigno (1987) and (1988); DiPhillips and Elliott (1987); Downie and Forshaw (1987); Gill (1987) and (1988); Kahan (1988); Manor (1991); McKechnie (1986a and 1986b); Shinman (1988) and Trowell and Huffington (1992). A book by Adamson and Warren (1983) describes the growth and functioning of one Children's Society centre. Some writers have outlined the development of family centres, explored their aims and potential and raised key issues: Cannan (1986); Hasler (1984); Holman (1987),(1992a) and

(1992b); B. Hudson (1989); Smith (1987); Thamesdown (1983); Walker (1991); and Warren (1986).

A study of some of the Children's Society's early family centres was undertaken by Phelan (1983). This provides an overview of twelve centres and some evaluation of eight of them. She notes the variations between centres and concludes that no two of the centres described were the same. The study indicates that the common focus of centres involves putting the child first, and seeking to help children to stay within their families and communities. The development of these family centres involved the Children's Society and its staff in incorporating new concepts and values into its work and this is true to some degree for any organisation and staff involved in establishing family centres.

Phelan concludes from her study that the three factors critical to the way a centre develops are:

(i)   how a centre is funded;
(ii)   what contractual arrangements are involved and;
(iii) who is appointed as project leader.

She indicates that centres do not have to conform to any particular pattern or model but that it is crucial that teams are clear about what they are doing and why and how they are doing it.

De'Ath (1985) reports on a study, commissioned by the Department of Health and Social Security, of self-help and family centres. Time and resource constraints of the project prevented any evaluation of the centres. The successes and the difficulties of centres were documented and the common features and differences noted. The report of the study, in addition to providing an overview of various self-help/family-centre initiatives, sought to promote discussion of a number of issues. 'Concern was expressed that "self-help" might become a political euphemism for the abandonment of government responsibility for the needs of families.' The study commented that if self-help family centres were to be developed they required resources and facilitation.

Holman (1988) sets a study of a number of voluntary projects in a context of the history of prevention in child care.

More than half the book explores development of the notion of prevention from Victorian times through the various landmarks of child care legislation to prevention in statutory and voluntary agencies in the 1980s. Holman notes the progress from the virtual absence of the concept in Victorian times to an expansion of the meaning of the word 'prevention' to the extent that he can identify eight different forms of prevention writing in the 1980s. In addition Holman advocates a greater emphasis on preventive services.

Many of the ten voluntary projects studied by Holman were family centres and all were Children's Society projects. Four projects are described in detail through the medium of interviews with the key people comprising staff, users, volunteers, and local authority social workers. Through his study, Holman identifies three different models of community projects. These he defines as:

● client-focused;
● neighbourhood;
● community development.

The majority of projects examined in Holman's study were described as falling within the neighbourhood/community development continuum.

Gibbons (1990) explores the purposes of family support and preventive services and examines the different approaches in two local authority areas. Family centres formed a significant part of one authority's services. The research provides a descriptive study of the family support projects and their impact on users and on the social services department's practice. Gibbons argues that neighbourhood-based projects are an effective way of a local authority fulfilling its responsibilities under the Children Act (1989) for the provision of family support. She suggests that such projects may best be provided indirectly by the local authority through resourcing voluntary and informal groups.

Cannan (1992) examines the development and nature of family centres. She explores how family centres represent the contradictions of social policy and the dilemmas of social welfare provision for families. Family centres are seen as part of the drive to emphasise family responsibility rather than collective responsibility for child care. The implications of such ideology, particularly in terms of restricted opportunities for women and children, are highlighted. The book includes material gathered both from research on ten family centres in southern England and from documents provided by several other centres of varied nature. Some comparisons with France are provided in terms of their social policy and French *centres socio-culturels*.

Cannan surveys the range of family centres and adds a category of service centre to Holman's threefold model. She outlines a framework of good practice for family centres which shows how they could 'realize their promise of supporting parents in the care of their children where they are in need, promoting better child-care in families and communities, and empowering their users' (Cannan, 1992, p. 119).

This is not a complete examination of literature on family centres and further reference will be made to various material at relevant points in other chapters. One common thread throughout all literature on family centres is the diversity of provision sharing the name family centre and this will be explored in the next chapter.

3

Models and Philosophies

The variety of provision

Goldberg and Sinclair (1985) after an examination of support services to families made the following comment about family centres:

> They vary widely in their aims, activities, and staffing patterns, in the type of family for whom they cater, in the degree to which they are involved in their local community and the type of communities they serve.

This observation is echoed throughout the literature on family centres as the last chapter demonstrated. Thus family centres may share a common title and yet vary enormously in their nature. Some centres may have more in common with establishments bearing different names such as children's centres or neighbourhood centres. Only limited assumptions can therefore be made about the services, participants, methods or staffing on the basis of the title 'family centre'.

As we noted in Chapter 2, several influences led to the evolution of family centres and the multiformity of centres is in part related to these influences. Thus whether a unit represents new provision, results from the closure of a home for adolescents or has evolved from a day nursery will have considerable implications for its population, staff and style. A range of factors, which contribute to the differences between centres, will be explored in this chapter.

Different philosophies

There may be significant contrasts in philosophies among centres. For example, some may view difficulties in child care and the risk or existence of child abuse as resulting primarily from the dysfunctioning of individual families. Other centres may understand the same problems in terms of failures in social structures, while yet others may hold an interactionist stance which sees problems as resulting from a complex inter-action between factors within the individual, the family and the wider social structures. Clearly such different perspectives will lead to diverse methods and approaches.

If the major contributing factors to child abuse are ident-ified as parental or family 'pathology' then a centre will focus its activities on the parents/family with the objective of chang-ing family functioning. If environmental conditions such as inadequate housing or lack of safe play facilities are viewed as significant causal factors then a centre's approach is likely to be based on a community development model. An interactio-nist philosophy is likely to lead to a combination of therapeu-tic and community development approaches.

Variety in philosophy will obviously lead to heterogeneity of goals pursued by centres. Garbarino (1982) makes a useful dichotomy in the nature of goals when he suggests that goals are either concerned with the minimisation of risk or with the optimisation of opportunities. This is closely allied to what he describes as the 'timing' of interventions which decides whether a service is preventive or remedial. As we saw in Chapter 2, prevention is best understood in terms of three levels: primary, secondary and tertiary (or remedial). There is diversity in terms of the level of prevention which centres believe to be their most appropriate concern and in the degree to which centres are concerned with the minimisation of risk or the optimisation of opportunities.

Common factors in centres

Before further exploration of the nature of differences between centres it is worth identifying and stressing the existence of common features. As De'Ath (1985, p. 7) comments:

> the phrase 'family centre' is increasingly being used as a generic
> term for any provision for parents and children where a range of
> services is offered to families living in a defined area and where
> the centre acts as a base for carrying out many of the activities.

Common factors among centres have been identified
through a number of studies by for example: Phelan (1983),
Hasler (1984), De'Ath (1985) and Holman (1988). It should
be recognised that in the main these studies tended to look at
voluntary sector centres and therefore some of the features
may not be associated with local authority centres. The elements identified were that centres:

● tend to be located in neighbourhoods of high stress where
  there is marked incidence of factors leading to the recep-
  tion of children into care;
● tend to draw out families' strengths rather than labelling
  them as a problem;
● tend to be accessible to local communities;
● work with parents as well as with children;
● emphasise user participation;
● have a commitment to increasing self-confidence and self
  esteem of users;
● provide a variety of services and activities for parents and
  children.

Categorisation of centres

A response to the considerable diversity found amongst
centres has led to various attempts to classify them. Some
examples of the different efforts at categorisation are given
below.

The Social Services Inspectorate (1986) suggested eight
descriptive categories:

1. Converted day nurseries.

2. Joint agency services for under fives.
3. Specialist non residential services for under fives.
4. Community/neighbourhood centres.
5. Multipurpose day centres.
6. Specialist day care.
7. Residential converted children's homes.
8. Residential special centres.

Downie and Forshaw (1987) suggest a twofold classification:

1. Neighbourhood-based community centres with an open, community-work orientation.
2. Centres for selected families, not open to all, with specific 'treatment' plans for individual families.

As indicated earlier, Holman (1988) provides three groupings:

1. Client-focused model.
2. Neighbourhood model.
3. Community development model.

The characteristics of a client-focused centre are its specialised activities, a concentration on work with referred clients, restricted neighbourhood outreach and professionalism rather than participation. The neighbourhood model Holman outlines as providing a broad range of activities, an open door, identification with the neighbourhood, local participation and flexible staff roles. The third model, community development, is characterised by indirect work, dissociation from traditional social work, collective action and local control.

The Department of Health (1991b) also provided a threefold system calling the three types:

1. *Therapeutic* 'in these, skilled workers carry out intensive casework with families experiencing severe difficulties with the aim of improving the ability to function as a family . . . Some such centres provide accommodation to do this.'
2. *Community* 'local voluntary groups including churches may

provide a neighbourhood based facility for parents to use as a meeting place and take part in particular activities.'

3. *Self-help* 'these may be run as a co-operative venture by a community group and are likely to offer various support services for families in an informal and unstructured way' (DoH, 1991, p. 19).

Warren (1990) propounds a typology 'in the light of the family and child care climate heralded by the Children Act':

1. Family support centres.
2. Community development centres.
3. Integrated centres.
4. Parentcraft centres.
5. Day care 'plus' centres.
6. Assessment and 'treatment' centres.
7. Creative residential centres.

Cannan (1992) suggests that family centres can be viewed as falling between two poles of social-work/child-protection or community-development/neighbourhood-centre. She concurs with Holman's classification but adds a fourth category, adapted from Walker (1991), of the service centre. The service centre 'is based on the assumption that the centre provides a service which directly benefits the users, that the service is one which they freely choose and in which they participate as much or as little as they wish' (Cannan, 1992, p. 31). Cannan sees this model as closest to the neighbourhood model but providing an emphasis on a professional service.

Every classificatory system sheds some light on the distinctions to be made between centres but each has limitations. Some centres can be allocated to a category immediately whilst others appear to fit several categories or none. Each fails to encompass the range of significant dimensions along which centres vary.

Dimensions for identifying differences between centres

An alternative to a simple categorisation is offered, through the development of a multidimensional schema. This identifies a number of variables through which family centres can be differentiated and compared. Individual family centres change over time and this identification of key components to family centres helps to recognise and evaluate changes.

A series of dimensions will be explored which can be used to distinguish centres from each other. Some of the factors which need to be considered when choosing between different positions on a dimension will be examined. The list is obviously not exhaustive but the following pivotal features have been selected:

1. Origins
2. Funding sources and sponsoring agencies
3. Context
4. Age of children
5. Referred families or open door
6. Target for intervention
7. Catchment area
8. Child or parent or family focus
9. Residential or day provision
10. Role of families in the centre
11. Staffing

1 Origins

As indicated earlier, centres come from differing origins. Some centres have slowly evolved from changing practice in day nurseries, others have involved the conversion of children's homes and the redeployment of staff. Many centres have been planned as new ventures.

The origins of some centres lie with local authorities, others have arisen from the change in emphasis of voluntary child care agencies and a minority of centres have been established from partnerships. Some partnerships have been between voluntary bodies and the local authority social services department whilst others have involved joint ventures between health and social services or education and social services.

In addition there are family centres whose origins rest with self-help groups such as Gingerbread or the Preschool Playgroup Association.

Factors to consider

A new venture has the clear advantage of the lack of previous history. Such a centre is usually set up in response to identified need and staff can be appointed with the skills to meet the nature and style of centre needed. In these circumstances it is often appropriate and feasible to involve the local community in plans for the new project. A disadvantage of a new unit can be that if the provision is needed urgently, the time involved in finding or building appropriate accommodation and in making the detailed plans, can lead to frustration for staff and for potential users.

An advantage of the conversion of existing provision is the converse of this disadvantage; the existing accommodation and the ready availability of redeployed staff can lead to a service being provided more immediately. However as Phelan (1983) concludes, 'changing an existing operation into a family centre is a long, difficult and disruptive process'.

The disadvantages of changing existing provision into a family centre arise from the difficulties associated with achieving effective change. The building may not be ideal, it takes considerable time for a changed identity to be recognised by outsiders and the centre's staffing may include individuals who have not chosen to work in a family centre except as an alternative to redundancy or some post to which they felt even less suited. The challenges of changing an existing establishment may be as great when the change is apparently minor as when it is sizable. Planning is needed as to how the changes are to be conveyed and implemented, for staff, current and future users and other agencies. Inherent conservatism which exists in most people and organisations can result in a denial of change and unconscious attempts to minimise the transformations required. It can be helpful to involve affected staff in identifying what is to be retained and what needs to be different.

Where there may be resistance by insiders and/or outsiders in acknowledging the changes required, ways need to be found of marking the distinctions; for example, by changing the name of the establishment and by a period of closure before opening as the family centre. Concern for the new service should not distract managers from the need to end and 'mourn' the old. Staff and users who have been part of an establishment are faced with feelings of loss when it is closed or changed and these need to be acknowledged and opportunities provided for them to be expressed and shared. Unless this essential work is done, staff will find it difficult to meet the challenges of the new provision.

2 Funding sources and sponsoring agencies

Phelan (1983) from her study of Children's Society family centres identifies the nature of a centre's funding as one of the biggest influences both on its instigation and its development. Cannan (1992) identified the policies of the local authority social services department and the enterprise of the voluntary child-care organisations as two of the main factors which create differences between family centres.

Family centres have a variety of funding sources and these may differ from the sponsoring agency and the centre's origins. This is particularly true of centres sponsored by voluntary bodies yet receiving a substantial amount of either local authority or central government finance.

In the main, centres tend to fall into one of four categories:

- Local authority centres
- Voluntary agency centres
- Joint ventures
- Self-help centres.

The funding source and sponsoring agency will both influence the nature of the centre. Thus Holman (1988) suggests that whilst some child care agencies may contain a larger number of client-focused centres, all the major voluntary child care agencies also include a large number of projects which fall into the neighbourhood- or community-development descriptions. In addition he noted that, although statutory and voluntary centres were not completely different creations, the majority of statutory centres were client-focused.

Factors to consider
Central government finance for family centres is invariably time limited. It is frequently an excellent source of 'start-up'

funding but leaves projects with major problems in securing longer term replacement revenue funds.

Centres sponsored by voluntary agencies carry the advantage of greater flexibility associated with the ability to take risks in innovating and experimenting. Their main disadvantage may be a recurrent uncertainty about finance. Conversely local authority centres often have less freedom but longer-term planning may be possible, although at times when major constraints operate on local government finance this latter advantage may not exist.

The development of contracts and service agreements may lead to voluntary organisations receiving funding from local government with very specific requirements about the family centre they provide. The advantage of such agreements is that there is greater clarity of expectation on both sides of the agreement. This can give greater security in funding terms, as it avoids the situation which has led to major problems for some centres when funds have been withdrawn without prior warning because the local authority has decided that the centre is not meeting the authority's priorities. The disadvantages are that it reduces the freedom of the voluntary agency and can restrict the degree of innovation and change its working style.

Joint ventures may offer access to two sets of resources, not only in terms of finance but also in terms of expertise and support services. However, not uncommon disadvantages are confusion about accountability and complex management issues arising from staff having different remuneration and conditions of service.

Self-help centres may offer great adaptability and greater freedom than any other model. There is always a danger that the model will be encouraged by central or local government primarily on a lowest-cost rather than a most-suited-to-need basis.

3 Context

Centres have distinct contexts made up of a number of components. The context includes the background to the development of the centre, its current funding and so forth. But in addition its context can be considered to include the nature of other provision in its environs. A centre on a new estate with no preschool services may identify the provision of day care or the promotion of child-minding as a high priority. A centre in a town centre well served by day nursery and nursery education is unlikely to share the same priority. Another centre may view the degree of preschool provision as having no direct bearing on the development of its services. The degree to which a centre is responsive to its context and the individual components to which the centre responds will differ from centre to centre.

Centres have to accept changing contexts. For instance, over time a centre may discover that its local population has altered because of changes in the local housing policy or that changing provision in the area – for example the establishment of a community health project – leads to a reduction in the need for certain of the project's services.

Factors to consider

A centre whose direction is determined more by 'internal' factors, such as its goals or staffing, will have more control over its evolution but may at a future time face overwhelming external pressures which threaten its existence.

However, a centre can be too responsive to its immediate context thus leading to constant change in its programme with resulting confusion for users and referrers.

4 Age of children

There are some centres which serve all families with dependent children and even households without children. But age-specialisation is common and tends to fall into the two groupings of preschool and secondary age. This is partially related to the origins explored earlier but a more fundamental principle underlies the origins. The two age-groupings reflect the fact that the distribution of ages of children looked after by the local authority peak at preschool and adolescence. This relates to the particular stresses which face families at these life stages.

Factors to consider

An advantage of specialisation is that families are concerned with different tasks and needs at preschool age and adolescence. Staff need different knowledge and skills to work effectively with these distinct age groups. The physical requirements in terms of building and equipment are notably disparate for the extremes of preschool and adolescence.

An obvious disadvantage of exclusivity of age range is that families frequently have children whose ages span a number of years. A recurrent issue for preschool-age centres is that of responding to families whose children have reached school age yet the parents still want and/or need some continuing provision but whose locality offers no particular support to parents of school-age children.

5 *Referred families or open-door*

Centres can be distinguished in terms of their referral policies. Certain centres focus their activity on referred families only, others have an 'open door' policy preferring to work with families who refer themselves. In some projects a mixture of referred families and self-referrals is encouraged. The source of referrals may differ, there being some centres which are set up primarily to work with families known to the local social services department and others which work mainly with families referred by health visitors.

Factors to consider

Stigmatisation is a major issue for centres who work with selected families. A review of one local authority's family centres reported that a phrase often heard from current and past users was 'It's the place you go when you bash your kids' (Buckinghamshire County Council, 1987). As a result, considerable thought and effort may need to be given to engaging families. In contrast, families who refer themselves to a centre are likely, in general, to have greater motivation for active involvement with the centre.

Working with selected families, particularly in times of limited resources, may ensure that scarce resources are targeted on families in greatest need. Centres operating an open-door policy may not attract families in most need of their resources. In describing the Banbury Family Centre, Smith (1987) states, 'Debate continues on how best to reach those families and children most in need with an "open access" service.'

6 Target for intervention

This has links with the previous dimension. A major distinction can be made between a therapeutic/client-focused model and a community-development approach. These can be viewed as at opposite extremes of a spectrum. There are also centres which seek to combine both approaches.

Factors to consider
As indicated when identifying differences in philosophy, decisions about the appropriate target for intervention rest on the definition of the problem. Focusing exclusively at either end of the spectrum may neglect important factors which are a major contributory cause of the problem being tackled.

Describing a client-focused centre Holman (1987) suggests 'The focus on a few families allowed a planned programme for each user using such skills as counselling, play therapy and group work.'

In the same article Holman comments on the advantages of a community-development approach:

> The benefits to be gained from the community development model were seen as threefold. Firstly, that the concentration on neighbourhood rather than individual needs conveyed no stigma. Secondly, that it enabled residents to develop their skills and confidence in order to have a greater say in shaping their own environments. Thirdly, less pressure on full-time staff as they were relieved both of the organisation of services and of intense counselling of individuals.'

Cannan (1992) indicates that the client-focused centre reflects organisational needs in a climate of emphasis on child protection. She suggests that it may also be preferred by staff as therapeutic approaches may be deemed, 'stimulating and prestigious compared to the more mundane business of supporting families in practical and educative ways' (Cannan, 1992, p. 111). But Cannan also provides evidence of families' preference for neighbourhood models and social workers' acknowledgement of the relevance of neighbourhood centres for their clients' needs. She urges centres to broaden their goals and provide 'greater opportunities for women, enriched lives for children through play schemes and daycare, which in their own way can reduce the stresses for families' (Cannan, 1992, p. 140).

Gill (1988) documents Fulford Family Centre's philosophy and practice of integrating therapeutic work with a community-work approach. The major benefits he records are, 'addressing the appropriate factors in the stress of individual families; encouraging participation; decreasing stigmatisation; aiding personal and group change'.

7 Catchment area

This is closely related to the two previous sections. A therapeutic approach tends to work with a wider catchment area and a community-based approach tends to work with a defined neighbourhood. Centres may vary between the extremes of those serving several towns with a total population of more than 100 000 and centres relating to a particular estate with a population of 1000. The defined boundaries may be flexible or not negotiable. Willmott and Mayne's study (1983, p. 121) found that:

> the boundaries of the catchment areas were, for some projects, constrained (if not imposed) by geographical considerations and for others by political ones. Other influences on defining areas were those of each project's purposes and their methods of recruitment of users.

Factors to consider

Willmott and Mayne's study noted that certain physical barriers can impose insurmountable problems but they can have a positive impact of delineating a very clear boundary and thus an obvious territorial identity for a project. The advantage of a restricted catchment area is the possibility of integrating the centre with appropriate networks both formal and informal.

Warren (1986) suggests that not all centres need to be neighbourhood-based:

> Many underorganised families present strong arguments to attend centres out of the neighbourhood . . . Labels and real difficulties for parents with major problems can mean that neighbourhood centres can exclude them. Hierarchies of 'copers' and 'non-copers' may emerge which may militate against serious involvement of families in centres.

Like many other features, the nature of the catchment area will relate to the aims of a centre. If the aims include encouraging mutual support amongst families then drawing the users from a wide catchment area will not serve such an objective. Tibbenham (1986) in his study of the West Devon Family Centre commented that the continued success of work with families rested heavily on 'phasing' them back into a more self-reliant situation in the community. But this task depended on staff building up a network of links in a local community and this was very difficult for a centre serving the whole town of Plymouth.

8 Child or parent or family focus

Centres differ in their focus of activity. Centres which provide a day-care service are likely to lean towards a child focus. Similarly centres working with adolescents and their families may define the adolescent as their client and work with families will be viewed as a subsidiary activity. Other centres may concentrate their services on parents, and activities for children will be more tangential. Some centres only work with whole families and their major focus may be family interaction, rarely providing separate activities for parents and for children. As indicated in the first chapter, parents and children sometimes have competing needs. Centres often have to seek a balance between these needs.

The extent to which fathers are involved in centres varies considerably. As indicated earlier, the providers of welfare services frequently assume that mothers are the prime carers of children and family centres may reflect such assumptions. Holman (1992a), summarising the benefits demonstrated by studies of family centres, comments:

> Women who attend the client-focused type centres learn child management skills in an environment which protects their children.

This suggests either that men do not attend client-focused centres or that they learn different skills. In fact there are centres which, when working with two-parent families, insist that both parents attend to learn parenting skills. Centres working with adolescents may find fathers easier to engage than preschool centres. Social expectations of fathers often include responsibility for the influence and control of older children but not the care of younger children.

Some of the predominance of mothers over fathers as participants in family centres may reflect particular demographic factors. Trowell and Huffington (1992) describe referrals to the Monroe Young Family Centre as including twice as many female adults as male because of lone parenthood. Gill (1992), in a study of forty families living in the vicinity of Fulford Family Centre, found nineteen lone-parent households with all but one being headed by a woman. Cannan (1992) states from her own and others' research that, 'lone parenthood features prominently amongst users of family centres' (Cannan, 1992, p. 120).

Factors to consider
In addition to the aims of a centre, the staff's training and background will have some influence on the target. Staff with nursery-nurse or teacher training may more readily take a child focus whilst staff trained in social work may tend towards a parent or whole-family focus.

Focusing solely on the child's needs, where parents also have pressing needs, may lead parents to 'compete' for staff attention and be surprisingly counter-productive in encouraging parents to meet their children's needs.

Focusing primarily on parents' needs can lead to neglect of the children's needs as, depending on age and developmental stage, they are frequently reliant on adults to articulate their needs.

Concentrating on the whole family to the point of parents always being with their children in a centre may deny parents the benefit for them and their children of some respite from child-care.

The involvement of mothers and fathers in centres is a crucial and complex issue and will be explored in the final chapter. For the purposes of this section a brief outline of factors will be provided. The structure of the family, in terms of one or two parents, is an obvious feature. The pattern of individual family roles and responsibilities should be considered and cultural and class differences must be recognised. Staff and parental attitudes need to be explored to identify sexist assumptions. As Holt (1992) warns, 'Family centres and social services departments may be seen by both parents and possibly by the worker as a women's place, created in women's time.'

The aims of a centre should be dominant in deciding a centre's approach to the involvement of men and women. Thus an aim to enhance parenting requires attention to both fatherhood and motherhood. As Walker (1991) points out, the neglect of the role of a father suggests that mothers are responsible for the existence and resolution of family difficulties. However a centre which is concerned with providing a refuge for women who are suffering domestic violence may view the participation of men as inappropriate.

Centres which encourage open informal groups, often of a parent/toddler composition, may find the centre gains an image of a women's place. Where women are active participants in a centre they may be ambivalent about the involvement of men. Eisenstadt (1986) recounts how mothers wanted the opportunity to be with other women. Women may find a centre a source of support and an arena where they can, for once, wield power and influence and they may be ambivalent or reluctant for men to be persuaded to attend.

9 Residential or day provision

The hours during which centres provide a service can vary between a few hours a week and a full-time residential service. The latter are in a minority but provide an important intensive service.

Factors to consider
The advantage of residential provision is that it can prevent unnecessary separation of the most vulnerable children from their parents and provide the opportunity of assessment over a prolonged period and at varied times and days. Centres which provide accommodation for individual family members in an emergency may help the family to negotiate a crisis effectively. A disadvantage of residential provision is that to some extent they create an 'unreal' situation in which to undertake assessment. It cannot provide a picture of the way that a family copes in the community with its particular pressures and stresses. Accommodating families away from their communities removes them from networks and makes it difficult for work to be done with the family on building up local supports.

A day family centre with restricted hours may not be open when families most need it. On the other hand it may encourage families to provide mutual support outside the centre's opening hours.

10 Role of families in the centre

The role undertaken by families in a centre varies and is linked to some degree to whether the centre is therapeutic/client-focused or carries some community-development focus. The differing roles can be defined as recipients of a service, participants in the service and controllers of the service.

Factors to consider
Recipients of a service may receive a highly skilled professional service but their definition as recipients may encourage

passivity, inequality and disempowerment. *Participants* may feel a greater sense of equality with other users and with staff but there may be lack of clarity as to the extent of their influence. *Controllers* will hold power, enabling families to influence decisions which greatly affect their lives. There may be difficulties in establishing effective and fair processes which define how (and which) parents become controllers of a centre.

11 Staffing

Staff are a key, and the most costly, feature of a centre. Staffing in centres varies in terms of size, qualifications, background, ethnic origin, gender and roles. Some centres may place priority on appointing a proportion of local people to the staff regardless of qualification whilst for other centres the nature of qualification and professional experience will be a vital attribute. The former will often be a feature of a community-development centre and the latter a concern for a client-focused centre.

Where staff are redeployed from establishments which have been closed, careful thought is needed. Individuals may have chosen employment in a children's home or day nursery because of their preference for working with children and may be reluctant to work with parents. Warren (1986) cautions, 'managers, honourably saving jobs, face serious difficulty in pressing people who have conventionally acted as home-makers and nursery nurses to become whole family workers.' Training and staff development are important issues for any family centre but are essential factors in preparing staff for a change of role. Stewart *et al.* (1990) in an article examining changing social work roles in family centres, quote a member of staff connected with a centre created from a former children's home:

> I think the biggest hiccup is that we've left it [the Family Centre] trying to function instead of shutting it down and reopening it. I think we tried to almost change overnight and leave them physically holding the baby of as many as eight adolescents at one stage, and expect them to train and develop themselves.

Factors to consider

Most family centres are concerned with parents and children and employ a range of methods. As a result they benefit from a staff team encompassing a mix of knowledge and skills which include:

a child orientation;

an adult perspective;

family and group dynamics;

a variety of methods and activities.

Issues of race must be considered, especially as there is often an under-representation of families from minority ethnic groups. In addition to issues of equal opportunities, an all-white staff group will be more likely to project an image of a white centre which is discouraging to users from different ethnic origins.

Gender is also a factor to recognise. As already stated, fathers are less involved in family centres than mothers and this is likely to be more marked if the staff group is all-female.

A more detailed exploration of staffing issues will be provided in a later chapter.

Creating profiles of family centres

The foregoing exploration of the many variables distinguishing centres from each other highlights the limitations of any simple categorisation of family centres. The identification of a number of dimensions on which an individual centre can be positioned allows a more detailed profile of a centre to be created. This not only allows centres to be compared but also, if used over a period of time, enables any major changes in an individual centre to be recognised. The most significant variables which can be expressed visually are as follows:

Sponsoring agency

Local authority	Voluntary agency	Self-help group

Funding sources

Central government	Local government	Voluntary agency	Charitable trusts	Fund-raising

Method of admission/selection of families

Referral from SSD only	Referral from various agencies	Referral from agencies and self-referral	Self-referral only

Focus of activity

Child	Family	Family in the community	Neighbourhood/ community	Social structures

Role of users

Recipients of centre services	Participants in centre	Controllers of centre

Other dimensions which can be added relate to some of the concepts explored earlier.

Type of prevention-timing

Tertiary	Secondary	Primary

Nature of goal

Minimisation of risk	Optimisation of opportunity
(Child protection)	(Child development)

The latter dimension may have parallels with a care and control dimension.

Methods used

Individual counselling	Family therapy	Groupwork	Community work

On some dimensions a centre can be pinpointed in one position, whilst on others a centre may be placed covering more than one point on the 'scale'.

An integrated model

The numerous variables explored in this chapter indicate how enormously and how subtly family centres may differ from each other. What is ideal, sadly, is too often unavailable because of limited resources and the influence of history. The exploration of factors to consider under each of the above sections tries to take account of the far-from-ideal world in which most family centres are established and operate. In times of constraint on resources and increasing emphasis on child protection, there may be pressures on family centres to move towards the left of each dimension. Thus centres may find themselves required to restrict their services to referred families where there are major concerns about parenting and actual or potential child abuse. This will be matched by an emphasis on tertiary prevention, the minimisation of risk, a target of child or family and not the neighbourhood. In such circumstances the families using the centres are more likely to be in the role of recipient rather than participant.

Different approaches each have their peculiar benefits and drawbacks. Yet, overall, cogent arguments can be presented for an integrated family centre model. The features of such an approach are as follows:

● *Open door policy* Referrals are accepted from all professional agencies and self-referrals are encouraged.
● *Several targets* The centre focuses not only on issues within the individual and his/her family but also on the structural
  and environmental components of the risks and opportunities facing families.
● *Neighbourhood base* The centre relates to a particular neighbourhood, thus enabling it to link with both the informal and the formal networks. This also facilitates a recognition of particular local pressures on families.

● *Combined focus* The centre recognises the individual needs of each family member but also addresses the family as a dynamic group.

● *Participants* The role of families using the centre is that of participants and not recipients. Families can not only be active in deciding the nature of their involvement in the centre but are also encouraged to influence the policy and practice of the centre. In some contexts it may be possible for families to move to a role of controller.

The advantages of an integrated approach are several. An open-door policy counteracts the powerful process of stigmatisation which so often occurs in centres restricted to referrals from professional agencies. It also recognises that families under stress do not always come to the attention of professional services and some may consciously avoid formal referral. An open door also encourages the involvement of a range of families each with their singular combination of strengths and vulnerabilities. Restricted referrals can lead to an unhelpful homogeneity of families who all being under particular and similar stress have limited resources to offer each other.

Selecting several targets for intervention, recognises the reality of the risks and opportunities which families face. As we have already indicated, the problems and potential that the majority of families face are neither restricted to their family functioning nor to their environment but to both.

A neighbourhood base encourages self-referrals and enables the promotion of informal networks. Research suggests that the extent and nature of support networks may be a significant factor in the quality of care a child receives (Polansky *et al.*, 1985).

The needs and fortunes of family members are closely intertwined thus it is more effective to address both the differing needs of children and parents and the interaction between them. Parents are able to provide a higher quality of child care when their own physical, social and emotional needs are being met. Children need experiences beyond their homes, they need relationships with other children and with adults who provide different models from their parents. If families are in conflict and disorganisation the interactions within the family also need addressing.

Families who use family centres often prefer to be called 'participants' rather than 'users'. This is both related to associations of 'user' with drugs and also to their concern to describe their relationship with a centre more accurately. Participation emphasises activity rather than passivity. It suggests the possession of some power and influence. It can also lead to a sense of partnership both between families and between families and staff. This latter relationship will be explored in a later chapter.

There is, as yet, very little research into the effectiveness of different centres in order to provide firm evidence as to the appropriateness of different models. What is needed is more evaluation which compares the outcomes of different centres and explores the relationship between aims and models.

4

Processes, Services and Resources

Stages and processes in family centre work

Work in a family centre whether concerned with the individual, family, group or community passes through a number of definable phases. These are as follows:

● Identification of need
● Contact
● Contract
● Assessment
● Implementing the contract
● Evaluation
● Termination

This is rarely a linear process but will include phases of circularity as worker(s) and participants continually assess, reassess and evaluate their work together. In addition there are some processes which run throughout the stages such as recording. However, for the purpose of clarity comments will be made about each of the stages and processes as though they were discrete entities.

All centres need to implement anti-racist policies in every stage and process. 'This is because anti-racist policies do not come into their own simply when assessing black children. They will inform every assessment, intervention and provision of service, even for white social workers who work exclusively with white families' (Macdonald, 1991, p. 72).

Identification of need

The ways in which a centre comes to work with a whole family, some family members, a group, or a formal or informal network varies. Crucial issues arise from how the need is identified. Three obvious sources exist:

● A member or members of a family may identify their need and approach a centre.
● The need may be identified by, or in conjunction with, other people who then approach (or play a central role in the family's approach to) the centre. Other people fall into two categories of formal or informal referrers. The first being other professional or helping agencies and the second tending to be family or friends.
● The centre may identify a general need and invite people to approach the centre. For example, a centre may identify the need for a group for adult survivors of sexual abuse and invite referrals from agencies and individual survivors. An example from a different level of system would be a centre's identification of the lack of safe play space in the neighbourhood.

In the first two sources the centre has to decide how to respond to a particular need brought to their attention. This requires a centre to be clear about its aims and objectives, which in turn leads to the definition of priorities. In the third approach the family centre has clearly decided that a particular need is a priority and that it has the resources to address the need.

Referrals to a centre provide the identification of individual or family need. It is important to families, staff and other agencies making referrals that there are both well-defined criteria and clear systems for making referrals. Effective publicising of the criteria and referral procedure is also essential. The criteria will emerge from the type and cover such points as whether there is a definite catchment area, whether referrals can be accepted from any source, and whether the age of the child(ren) is a determining factor.

Most centres will assist the referral process by the development of referral forms. A central issue surrounding referral from other agencies is whether the form, or any other vehicle for referral, fully involves the family in its completion. Such full involvement helps the family, in this earliest stage of their introduction to the centre, to have some influence and control and to have some awareness of the purpose of the referral and the expectations of the referrer. One way of encouraging this approach is for a centre to require that referral forms are completed and signed by referred and referrer.

Extensive involvement of the family in the referral procedure avoids *hidden agendas*. A hidden agenda occurs where a referrer feels unable to express his/her real concerns to a family and gives them a different version of the reason for referral. For example, without a jointly completed form the family centre may be told that the referrer has serious unease about the parenting skills of the parents but the family has been told that the centre would be a useful place to go to make friends. The Children Act and developments in more open practice in all professions should make hidden agendas a problem of the past.

All centres need to give thought to ethnic monitoring in their referral process. This is important in terms of exploring with an individual family their racial and cultural origins and any implications in terms of appropriate services. It is also vital for providing information as to the extent black families are using a centre and whether or not they are under-represented when referral statistics are compared with local demographic data.

The allocation of referrals needs consideration. Inevitably this is about matching resources to needs and frequently the ideal cannot be achieved. There are many arguments for team allocation and the value of teamwork will be explored later. Genuine team participation avoids the styles of allocation encountered by Parsloe (1981) and described as 'by the senior alone, "the drop it on their desks at night method" and by discussion (or silence) at a team meeting "the eyes-down method"' (Parsloe, 1981, p. 59).

Contact

How the earliest stages of contact are managed may be a crucial factor in engagement and thus in the effectiveness of the work undertaken. Some of the issues to be considered are: Who should be the participants in the first meeting? How many family members should be involved? For example, if the mother and child(ren) are being referred yet there is a partner mentioned should not the partner also be included? The referrer may not have had contact with the father/stepfather and may be making assumptions about responsibilities for parenting which the family centre needs to question. Failure to recognise individuals who are part of the family system, in the earliest stages of contact, can impair future work with the family.

Is the referrer to be present at the first meeting with the family? Is the meeting to take place in the family centre or the family's home? Is the initial contact to be arranged directly by the family centre worker or through the referrer? There are arguments for and against the possible answers to each of these questions. Some of the factors influencing the decisions will be the characteristics of the family and their need, the family's relationship with the referrer and the centre's relationship with the referrer.

Some centres providing informal services may find it effective for current or previous centre participants to be involved in making early contacts with a new referral.

Contract

The notion of a contract can be applied to most if not all work in a family centre although the degree of formality or explicitness will vary considerably. The advantages of contracts are that they encourage clarity about the aims of any piece of work and about the responsibilities and expectations of all the participants, including of course the centre worker(s). In some circumstances it may be important to have a clear written contract, such as the written agreements emphasised by the Children Act 1989.

The contract-making stage may take a number of sessions

with a parent or family as, together with the worker, they explore their needs and the ways in which the centre and its workers might assist in meeting the needs. It is always important to work at the user's pace. Where individuals are ambivalent about change, or because of past experiences doubtful of any worker's ability or willingness to assist, it may need considerable persistence and patience to engage the potential participants.

Where working with a whole family or a group there will need to be both individual aspects and family or group aspects to any contract. Depending on the nature of the referral, a contract may need to include different views and expectations. Thus, if a social worker refers a family for assessment of their parenting skills the contract might include both the referrer's and the family's definition of their problem and their different expectations of what the family might get from the centre. When a family is required to attend it is vital that this is explicit and that feelings of resentment and reluctance are acknowledged and explored.

The following areas need to be included:

(a) individual participants' assessment of their need/ difficulties;
(b) individual participants' assessment of their strengths and resources;
(c) referring agencies' (if not a self-referral) assessment of need/difficulties currently experienced by the individual/ family;
(d) referring agencies' assessment of strengths and resources possessed by the individual/family;
(e) a definition agreed between individual participants and centre staff of need/difficulties and strengths and resources of the family;
(f) agreed aims and goals for change; some thought needs to be given to how the attainment of the goals is to be demonstrated and measured.

Other information would include participants in the work, activities to be undertaken, frequency of attendance, estimated duration of work, frequency of and arrangements for reviews.

A centre will also have either implicit or explicit contracts with some referring agencies. These may relate to the overall work of the centre but will carry implications for work with each and every family. In many instances there will be more specific agreements relating to work with individual families. Such agreements will obviously need to be congruent with the centre's contract with the family.

Assessment

This is a recurrent activity throughout work with an individual, family, group or neighbourhood and is present from the earliest phase. It is in the forefront during the early stages of contact but continues until work is completed. It is important that workers continually re-examine their hypotheses and assumptions about a situation and alter them in the light of later knowledge and understanding.

A thorough assessment includes both breadth and depth. The needs and resources of the family or group are identified in detail and the wider context and its influences are examined. In making assessments workers will be applying a particular framework of knowledge and theory drawn from several disciplines. Assessment may be assisted by the use of a structured guide which identifies the areas and dimensions which need to be explored. Kahan (1988) provides an example of guidelines used for observing and assessing parents with young children in a residential family centre. Reith (1979) provides a useful assessment guide devised by a Family Service Unit for work with families. This takes into account aspects of the individual, the family and the community and explores both strengths and stresses. Reith points out that an assessment guide 'helps to inform professional judgement, but it is not a substitute for it.' He also gives apposite warnings, which apply to the use of any assessment guide, first, about the dangers of overlooking the dynamic nature of family functioning and second, the danger of 'labelling' a family rather than recognising its unique strengths and difficulties.

In undertaking assessments white workers must be aware of the dangers of applying Eurocentric values and norms. As Ahmed *et al.* (1987) counsel, 'expecting diversity, social workers must learn what is important for the people with whom they work by careful observation, by listening and by asking their consumers who are, of course, the experts.'

Many family centres will be requested to provide an assessment of a family in order for critical decisions to be made about a child's future. Thus a child-protection case conference or a court may be the source of a request for assessment. In such circumstances the assessment will need to be rigorous and the use of guidelines will be particularly relevant. The Department of Health document (1988), *Protecting Children* provides a comprehensive framework for undertaking assessments for long-term planning in child-protection cases.

Dale *et al.* (1986) describe a team approach to assessment in child protection which is highly structured, preferring to work within the mandate of a statutory order and emphasising the team's authority. Dale (1991) subsequently describes a very different style of team assessment by another NSPCC team which is structured and comprehensive but encourages voluntary participation by a family.

The Race Equality Unit (1990) provides a positive code of practice which enables organisations and workers to address issues of race and ethnicity in child protection.

Implementing the contract

The way in which the participants fulfil the contract will depend on the approaches and methods used. Later sections in this chapter and the next chapter are assigned to this phase of work.

Evaluation

Evaluation is an essential aspect of all family centre work and wider issues concerned with evaluation of a centre's work will be discussed in Chapter 8. Evaluation should be built in as a routine component of the work with individual families and groups. Such an incorporation of evaluation allows an assessment of the extent of change in the particular family or group and it also allows the family or group members in question to play an equal part in decisions about the work. If meaningful evaluation is to be achieved then, as indicated above, a clear assessment of need and explicit setting of goals should have been undertaken in the earliest stages of contact and contract.

Evaluation then takes place at each point of reviewing the work with the family or group. At this stage the following are then explored together:

(a) current position of family in terms of need/difficulties;
(b) current level of strengths and resources of the family;
(c) progress, or lack of progress towards attainment of goals agreed in the contract;
(d) views on the methods and approaches used; what helped and what hindered? This should include aspects of the workers' performance.

Whilst evaluation should take place throughout the work with the family it will be more extensive in the final stages of contact.

Termination

Endings are an inevitable and important part of a centre's work whether with individuals, families or groups. This phase of involvement needs careful thought and planning. In neighbourhood centres where an individual or family can participate in many different activities there may be a gradual series of endings as they separate from various services before the family eventually ceases any active connection with the centre. This may feel like an encouraging 'growing away' from the centre as the parent or family becomes engaged in other tasks and activities. It is still important that each ending is recognised appropriately. In centres where a family may have only one, though intensive, form of involvement there may be a more condensed and obvious termination.

The termination stage engenders a range of feelings in both participants and staff. These may be ambivalent, with a family both valuing the change in their circumstances and experiencing sadness at 'moving on'. Just some of the reactions common to an ending phase are: denial, sadness, a recurrence of former difficulties or the emergence of new problems, anger, gratitude, relief, and a sense of achievement. A participant's response to the ending phase will be influenced by previous experiences of separation and loss and the impact of past unresolved losses needs to be addressed. Termination should never be sudden and unplanned and thus an individual or family will be prepared for it and their feelings acknowledged. Obviously individuals or families themselves may terminate their participation prematurely and in an unplanned way; one reason for this occurring is where previous endings have left a legacy of unresolved distress and anger. On such occasions it may be important that the worker(s) acknowledge the termination as a valid decision and explore the reasons for it with the participants, rather than letting things drift to an unclear end.

The reasons for endings and the resultant mix of feelings will vary. The most positive and easiest scenario to manage is where family and centre agree that the goals of participation have been achieved. Often there will be less complete agreement and the reality of scarce resources may sometimes mean that a centre has to instigate or encourage parting before the individual or family fully desires it. Thus centres whose primary focus is on children under five years of age may find that the parents want to continue to participate in centre activities after their children have started school, but if they remain involved this may result in the centre being able to take on fewer families with children under five.

Termination is likely to be more effective, in the sense of achievements being carried forward, where some work is done on how the individual/family is going to consolidate and build on what they have achieved. As Butler and Elliott (1985, p. 55) observe:

> the most constructive way to work with endings and losses, of whatever kind, is fully to experience the events, integrate them, acknowledging the feelings aroused; and then let go (without forgetting) so as to move forward into the future.

Recording

Recording is an activity which needs to take place through all phases of the work. Kahan (1988, p. 15) comments:

> Records in social work, though an important part of the social work task, are frequently the subject of adverse comment in research studies, government inspections and public inquiries . . . Yet records are vitally important to the client and his future . . . To be of value they must be up-to-date, accurate, regular, and systematic and this implies a commitment and discipline which recognises their importance.

All centres need to have a policy of open records and this encourages clarity about the purpose and relevant content of any written files. Records completed jointly by the individual/family/group and worker can form a useful tool as part of both the intervention and evaluation. Thought should be given to how individuals with literacy problems can be involved in a recording process. Forms for recording encourage some consistency and continuity in the information recorded by the team.

Records of group meetings may be used by groups to develop their cohesion by assisting their recall of previous sessions.

Example 4.1

A parents' group would start each of its meetings by reading the worker's account of the previous session. The record included reference to individuals and accounts of discussions which contained both painful and hilarious topics. Members would then enlarge on the contents for other members who had been absent on the previous occasion. The ritual of reading the record both reintegrated absent members and encouraged individual members by the worker's written acknowledgement of their contribution to the group.

Range of activities and services

The number and range of activities in a centre will, as with so many other features, depend on the model of centre. The centre programme should evolve from the centre's aims, objectives and priorities. Warren (1986) states, 'a crucial characteristic has been the way family centres have laid on a varied menu of activities for parents and in my view this aspect is at the core of the movement and accounts for their effectiveness'.

A recurrent issue for most centres when firmly established is how to develop new and necessary activities when existing resources are fully committed and no additional resources are available. Clearly the only way developments can take place is at the expense of existing activities but such decisions are exacting and unpopular.

There is no categorisation of the activities and services of family centres which is both simple and comprehensive. For the purpose of analysis five categories are suggested:

1. Advice/advocacy about rights/obtaining resources
2. Direct provision of resources
3. Work with individuals and families
4. Work with groups
5. Community work/development.

The next chapter will concentrate on the last three categories and the remainder of this chapter will consider aspects of advice/advocacy and the provision of resources.

Advice and advocacy

The examples of rights and resources which will be used are probably those most frequently a focus for a family centre's advice or advocacy work – family rights, and welfare rights.

Often in advocacy work the aim of a centre will be to facilitate self-advocacy and thus to empower the individual or group to obtain their rights. As Croft and Beresford (1991) urge:

Support people to speak for themselves. Individual and collective self-advocacy offers people the most effective way of getting the services they need, the changes they want and their rights.

Family rights

The two aspects of family rights which centres are likely to address are children's rights and parents' rights. Franklin (1986) suggests that the complex range of children's rights can be clustered into two groupings: protective rights and self-determination rights. The former covers the Rights of the Child expressed in the United Nations Declaration covering such aspects as nutrition, housing, medical services and education. This category also includes the right of the child to protection from, in Franklin's words, 'inadequate care, neglect and physical or emotional abuse in the home, or any other form of danger' (Franklin, 1986, p. 14). The second category is concerned with children having greater autonomy and influence over various parts of their lives. The Children Act's emphasis on the child's wishes is some small movement towards this kind of right.

From this brief outline of children's rights it should be readily apparent that there are many ways in which family centres can be advocates for children. In consideration of a child's protective rights many centres take an active role in campaigning for children's rights and needs both locally and nationally. Thus centres may be prime movers in pressing for better housing or safe play areas for children in a locality. Both parents and staff may participate in efforts to publicise the needs of children and families such as promoting locally a national petition for better transport facilities for parents with young children.

Frequently centres will be advocates for the right of children to be protected from neglect or abuse. Some activities which reflect this approach include:

— 'no smacking' rules in a centre;
— educative approaches with groups of parents as to the causes and effects of physical, sexual or emotional abuse;

- encouraging the effective parenting and nurturing of children;
- involvement in child-protection procedures when it is apparent that a child is at risk of abuse;
- urging that a different placement be found for a black child who is looked after by the local authority and whose ethnicity is being neglected.

Centres also may be concerned with self-determination rights for children. They will practise this in their work with children by involving them wherever possible in choices and decisions which affect them. They may act as advocates for children by pressing for a child's wishes to be discovered and taken into account in decisions made by social services or the child's school.

Family centres also have a role in parent advocacy. Warren (1990) researching the potential role in family centres concluded that they were well-placed to undertake parent advocacy. The Children Act has shifted a legislative focus from parents' rights to parental responsibility and also carries the assumption that parenting is for life. Parents may need advocacy to assist their parental responsibility which could involve for example:

- seeking contact with a child who is looked after by the local authority;
- providing the venue for contact to take place;
- accompanying a parent to court.

Welfare rights and advocacy

Why and how?
A family centre provides an appropriate setting for a welfare rights and advocacy service. This is especially so where the centre is accessible to its local neighbourhood, but is true also of more client-focused centres. Where a centre wishes to expand its service to a wider range of families, the addressing of welfare rights problems is an ideal way to facilitate this.

Arguments for a centre's involvement in the financial and material difficulties of its users both individually and collectively are several. The overwhelming majority of family centre participants are likely to be either claimants of state benefits or living on a low wage. They are also likely to be experiencing the exercise of power by a number of agencies including benefits agencies, fuel boards, housing authorities, the courts and others over vast and basic areas of their lives. Whether a centre's fundamental concerns are with empowerment or with the freedom from abuse of its youngest users, or with any number of points between these concerns, the realities of poverty and power exert an unremitting influence on the achievability of any of the centre's goals.

Obviously advice and advocacy alone will no more alleviate poverty than the resources of social work will eliminate the abuse of children. One fundamental aim of advice and advocacy services is to assist particular families to maximise their income. Simultaneously there can be a small redressing in the balance of power in their dealings with the large agencies that exercise so much control over their quality of life. For such a service to be effective it is helpful for it to be offered on a regular and publicised basis, so that potential consumers are clear when and where it takes place and who is involved. In addition to such a regular service there is always likely to be the need for emergency advice and advocacy.

Where advice work is part of the core of a centre's services it is easier to develop a common approach and detailed policies accepted by all workers, whether or not they directly contribute to the service. Such policies would include when and how applications should be made to charitable trusts. It may be quicker to apply to a charity but important first to tackle the Department of Social Security. Similarly, it may be simpler for the worker to telephone a particular agency but much more effective for the individual if they are enabled to 'put their own case' with the worker remaining available to assist.

The life of most centres revolves round groups, which greatly contributes to the relevance of the setting to advice and advocacy work. Participants' common experiences of inadequate benefits, low wages and high-handed treatment by many agencies, combined with meeting each other and staff as a group or groups, provides opportunities to meet needs in ways beyond the provision of individual advice or advocacy.

Generalising individual users' experiences enables people to assist their needs collectively against systems which consistently deny them. Examples of this would be facilitating the discussion of benefits problems, changes in the law, or general issues of poverty. The settings for such discussions might be a drop-in, a support group, or the coffee break in a parenting group. First, this approach encourages the sharing of experiences and this begins to break down the individualisation of poverty which the benefits system creates. Second, it provides opportunities to challenge those familiar myths about the outrageously generous way the system has treated other individuals. Third, feasible collective responses can be generated and pursued.

Example 4.2

Fulford Family Centre was greatly concerned about the effect of the introduction of the Social Fund on families with small children. This had further impoverished families on Income Support and increased their dependency on other agencies. Most charities demand that social workers or health visitors are intermediaries between themselves and their beneficiaries and thus families are dependent on professionals' willingness and availability to help them to obtain charitable grants. Indeed to have basic needs met through the caprice of individual charities, rather than through public agencies' recognition of rights, is a major step in the direction of increased dependency. A centre worker facilitated participants in their sharing of experiences and discussion of possible actions to exert pressure on their local Department of Social Security office to modify the operation and interpretation of criteria for Community Care grants. As a result publicity and a petition were organised.

A decision to provide a welfare rights service as a discrete component within a family centre carries with it an associated decision as to the scope of the service. Thus, will it be restricted to the centre's existing or potential users or will it carry a wider responsibility?

Example 4.3

A decision was made early in the development of Fulford Family Centre to establish a specific time during the week for welfare rights advice. This was partly to establish some control over requests from users for advice and partly also to extend the service beyond regular users to potential users. A decision then had to be made as to whether the service should be available to residents who were not within the centre's terms of reference. It was decided that it would be available to all residents as there would be difficulties in advertising an advice service limited to a narrowly defined group. In practice, the majority of users of the service were parents with young children. An advantage of the more extended service was that it provided a broader understanding of neighbourhood issues which equally affect the major users of the centre.

The involvement of users in the decisions relating to the provision of a welfare rights service is likely to be influenced by their knowledge of such a service.

Example 4.4

The centre set up a welfare rights committee comprising one worker and a small group of parents to provide a forum for exploring issues related to the welfare rights service. The parents rapidly made it known that they needed some basic knowledge in order to participate. A basic welfare rights course was arranged, as a consequence of which some parents began to contribute to the advice sessions.

The above illustration raises the question as to whether the outcome resulted in parents being empowered or exploited as unpaid labour. This issue will be explored later from a broader basis.

Provision of resources

Resources provided by family centres can be considered under three headings of practical resources, buildings and people.

Practical and material resources

Family centres often offer practical services or share their material resources with families. It is relevant at this point to quote some of the findings of the Barclay Report (1982) about clients' views of social workers. Having outlined the satisfaction of a large number of clients, the Report continues:

> On the other hand, there is another clearly identifiable group who consider that social workers fail to provide the material things or practical help and advice which they desperately need . . .

The provision of practical resources may be a response to the poverty and deprivation experienced in an area.

Example 4.5

A profile of the neighbourhood, produced prior to the centre opening, revealed the absence of a launderette in the vicinity. As a result Fulford obtained funding to install a washing machine and tumble-drier for the use of local families.

The same centre, fairly soon after opening, received frequent requests for the use of the telephone as the nearby public one was constantly out of order due to vandalism. The centre subsequently arranged for the installation of a payphone within the centre.

Some facilities may enable individuals or families to fulfil duties which otherwise would be extremely difficult and therefore in danger of being ignored. For example, the management of debts and payments of fines can be hampered when recipients are an expensive journey away and the debtor has no bank account.

Example 4.6

Families' disclosures of debts and fines and their practical difficulties in making payments resulted in the centre opening a special bank account. Each week an individual could bring in one cash sum and instruct the centre to make a number of cheque payments to offset various debts or fines.

The combination of poverty and the physical isolation of a neighbourhood can result in its inhabitants enjoying little variety in their lives. Children may grow up with lamentably limited experiences. A centre's arrangement of outings and holidays can provide new experiences for children and break the otherwise monotonous routine for parents. Holidays may be offered on an individual or group basis. A group holiday provides considerable scope for unfamiliar experiences in novel environments for both children and parents. New friendships can be forged and mutual support discovered. Children will benefit from the more extensive and intensive contact with other adults in addition to their parents. Organising events in the local neighbourhood, such as a travelling theatre or hiring an inflatable, can also extend horizons and supply some enlivening entertainment for families whose disadvantage prevents access to most sources of amusement.

The provision of basic necessities such as food may carry significance beyond the satisfaction of physical need. Lunches or snacks may be very important to families both in helping their stretched budgets but also symbolically as emotional 'feeding', offering the nurture of care and concern. Centres may find food a central unifying theme in many groups, such as a food-allergies group, or a healthy-eating group or cookery

groups. Families may assist each other with some basic resources such as setting up a 'nearly new' clothing store.

Knowledge and information are essential resources which
centres can provide and facilitate families in sharing. A philosophy of partnership will mean that staff share their knowledge and skills rather than wanting to protect their expertise.
A centre may obtain books and videos on child care or health
issues and make these available for parents to borrow.

The building and equipment

As indicated above, both the building and its equipment may
be valuable resources to users and the wider neighbourhood.
Buildings are often far from ideal and it demands imagination
to make the most of them. Advantages and disadvantages are
found in most types of buildings. Purpose-built buildings offer
freedom to design the environment to suit the requirements of
the centre but converted houses or flats can offer more informal and familiar surroundings. Wherever possible users
should be involved in the choice of décor, furniture and
equipment. Criteria that usually need to be considered are
durability and comfort. An anti-discriminatory policy will
also inform the creation of a centre's physical environment,
ensuring its physical and psychological accessibility to men
and women, adults and children, black and white, people with
disabilities and those who are able-bodied.

Contact, whether with children who are looked after by the
local authority or who are with a separated partner, can be
difficult to arrange and manage. A family centre can provide a
neutral and 'child-friendly' territory for such visits.

A centre may have equipment and materials which families
are encouraged to use. Many centres set up toy libraries but
other equipment may be borrowed such as decorating or
carpentry tools. Resources may be shared with groups as well
as with individuals. Thus the building or its equipment may
be made available to self-help groups.

People

The major human resources in family centres are staff, users, and volunteers. The first two categories will be considered in later chapters.

Volunteers and family centres
Volunteers have a long and valued tradition as a vital re-source in social welfare provision. In a family centre volunteers may fulfil a variety of roles and their introduction to a centre may be through a number of different routes. As the Barclay Report (1982) stated:

> Engaging and using volunteers satisfactorily and within their familiar situations is a sensitive and skilled task.

This requires a commitment of staff time and one effective way of achieving this is to appoint a volunteer organiser or at least to confer responsibility for volunteers onto one member of staff.

Successful volunteering is based on a reciprocal relationship where both volunteers and the service in which they engage are beneficiaries. The nature of volunteers has changed through the years and it is now well-recognised that voluntary service is not solely a middle-class activity. The reasons for volunteering are many and cannot be explored in detail here. However, the individual needs of volunteers must always be recognised if they are to be successfully deployed. In times of high unemployment the number of potential volunteers greatly increases. Thus volunteers may be looking both for constructive and fulfilling activities and the possibility of using or gaining skills.

Family centres gain a number of things from volunteers in addition to their time and skill. If volunteers are from the local neighbourhood the centre may be assisted in its links with informal networks. On the other hand volunteers from other areas may offer objectivity and anonymity which some users may desire.

Recruitment and selection A multiplicity of methods exists for the recruitment of volunteers. The most appropriate will depend on the kind of volunteer sought and whether or not local volunteers are desired. Some neighbourhood-based centres pursue a policy of only seeking local volunteers as part of a philosophy of building up mutual support and skills within an area. Posters, newspaper articles, leaflets through doors, addressing local groups, and the use of local radio or television are some of the obvious channels for contacting potential volunteers. Fulford's experience was that the use of regional television produced an enormous response and mostly from the very immediate vicinity, whereas months of pursuing other methods had led to disappointingly few enquiries.

A set procedure for the selection of volunteers is important and a centre needs to be clear about the criteria and methods they use to assess suitability. A simple form will provide basic and standard information about volunteers and usually it is helpful to take up some references. Where volunteers are undertaking work with children then it is essential that police checks are carried out. Such a process can seem a long one to the prospective volunteer who may have an expectation that s/he will start on the day interest is expressed. However, such procedures both ensure that children are in contact with people who are safe, reliable and committed and also it assists in raising the status of volunteering. The inevitable delay may lead to difficulty in maintaining people's interest but this can sometimes be overcome if the procedures and the reasons for them are fully explained and if initial induction and training is provided.

Training and support for volunteers is essential and the form of the training programme will clearly arise from the function of the volunteer(s). Induction to the centre is a vital component so that the volunteers feel part of the place and understand where their contribution fits into the wider picture. Group meetings for volunteers for training and support enable a sharing of ideas and skills and the facilitation of mutual support.

Users as volunteers   Many centres encourage current or former users of a centre to become volunteers. Some projects may restrict the recruitment of volunteers to centre participants. As the Barclay Report urged:

> We do not feel that clients should be seen simply as recipients of a service, therapy or care. It is important that they are all regarded as potential 'volunteers' (Barclay Report, 1982, p. 78).

The principle of users as volunteers is clearly in keeping with a philosophy of participation and partnership. Their experience as users can be of considerable benefit to a centre and the role of volunteer can enhance confidence and self-esteem.

Pertinent issues in a centre's use of volunteers The supply of and demand for volunteers is often ill-matched; either suitable volunteers are not available when needed or people offer involvement which cannot be utilised. Strategies for managing both circumstances need to be developed.

Confidentiality is an issue which may need emphasis and is highlighted particularly where volunteers from the local neighbourhood are recruited. Where volunteers are working directly with children they will need some awareness of child protection and which staff they must speak to if they have any concerns relating to the protection of a child.

Volunteers may have times of personal stress and difficulty and during such periods require additional support. Where volunteers are also current or past centre users there can be an issue about who should provide the support. If the centre has a volunteer organiser s/he may be the regular source of support for volunteers but if a volunteer previously received assistance from another member of staff they may seek further help from them. It can be important to clarify roles and responsibilities in such an event.

Volunteers provide a vital resource to many centres and their effective involvement requires commitment and interest from all staff.

As this chapter indicates the processes, services and resources within a family centre can be many and various.

5

Approaches and Methods in a Family Centre

Some social work writers have used a systems perspective in their efforts to synthesise the multiple theories and practice of social work (Specht and Vickery, 1977). The resultant 'unitary approach' emphasised the common aspects of what previously had been treated as quite disparate methods. This stance would view work with individuals, families, groups or communities in terms of intervention at different levels or systems. For the purposes of this chapter the methods and approaches used in family centres will be considered under the traditional headings which can be viewed as both levels/ systems for intervention and methods of work.

Context and choice of method or approach

Before exploring issues associated with the application of each method within a family centre, some general comments will be made about the relevance of different approaches and the influence of a family centre context.

As indicated in Chapter 3, family centres vary in the focus of their work and this in turn influences the degree to which they work at the varied levels of intervention or utilise different methods. As part of research to examine the potential for parent advocacy in family centres, Warren (1990) obtained information about 352 family centres. His results, summarised in Table 5.1, showed the percentage of family centres using different types of intervention.

The methods employed by any centre should relate to the

Table 5.1

Type of intervention	% of centres
Counselling	92.6
Groupwork	84.7
Community development	51.1
Family therapy	46.6
Psychotherapy	6.0

aims of the centre and the needs of the particular families that comprise the centre's target population. Thus a centre whose aim is to improve the environment for local families will clearly be utilising community development approaches. Centres whose objectives include improving family functioning may employ counselling/psychotherapy, family therapy and group-work.

The nature of a family centre means that certain methods and techniques are incongruent with the underlying values, philosophy and structure. An immediate example of this would be a psychoanalytic approach to either individual or group-work which discourages contact between worker and client(s) or between group members between contracted sessions. Most centres involve staff and family members in a complex matrix of overlapping relationships. In the majority of instances this in itself is viewed as beneficial and is encouraged. Therefore an approach that sets strict limitations to contact would be unacceptable as well as being impracticable to follow. An example of a specific technique which would appear to be in conflict with most centres' concern with openness and honesty would be the use of paradox as pursued in some family therapy approaches.

A text such as this, looking at all aspects of family centre work, cannot go into much detail about particular approaches and many sources are available which provide comprehensive information about the theory and application of different methods. Thus the remainder of this chapter will be selective and concentrate on specific issues which surround work with individuals, families, groups and neighbourhoods from a family centre base.

Working with individuals

Different traditions and approaches

Contact with a range of centres suggests that it would be unusual to find a centre adhering solely to one particular therapeutic approach to individuals and families. Most centres are eclectic, drawing on a wide range of insights and techniques and applying them to their specific setting. There are a number of sources of information about different approaches – for example, Nelson-Jones (1982) and Kovel (1983). The aim and need of the individual should be the determining elements in selecting an approach. Staff will have their own preferences for particular approaches and will have developed their own individual style of work which is likely to have emerged from a combination of their personality, values, background, training and experience. If a staff team is fortunate enough to contain members who favour different approaches then there is the possibility of matching the individual/family need and the aim of intervention with a particular approach and style.

Counselling

Work with individuals may be described in varied ways. Most frequently such work is defined as either counselling or psychotherapy. As indicated earlier, Warren's (1990) research showed the vast majority of family centres reporting that they undertook counselling. In comparison a very small number indicated that they practised psychotherapy. Whilst certain clear distinctions can be made it has to be acknowledged that the two approaches overlap. Both may be concerned with the person's internal and external worlds and with the interaction between them, and also with the dysfunctional impingement of past experiences onto the present. The relationship between counsellor/therapist and the individual is central in both approaches. In the main, psychotherapy focuses more on the internal world and on the 'transference' which involves the responses to significant childhood figures that the individual transfers to his/her relationship with the worker.

Although few centres may define themselves as practising psychotherapy, some of the insights offered can be particularly useful. Understanding the nature of transference and counter-transference can assist workers in making sense of what may otherwise appear to be inexplicable feelings or irrational behaviour on the part of the user or the worker. The importance of reliability and consistency in the therapeutic relationship, expressed concretely by such things as a regular time for meeting and the protection of sessions from interruptions, are principles that can be helpfully pursued.

Any consideration of different approaches to counselling or therapy benefits from a reminder of research findings. Examination of varied 'schools' of therapy/counselling described by Truax and Carkhuff (1967) identified three key features which appeared to be common to effective practice. These characteristics were:

(i)   accurate empathy;
(ii) non-possessive warmth;
(iii) genuineness.

Workers may sometimes misguidedly believe that the development of more sophisticated techniques would most enhance the service provided whereas a greater development of the above characteristics would best serve the 'clients'.

Who is counselling for?

The aims of many family centres are concerned with children and many of their direct services, as explored later, will be addressing the needs of children. It is important to keep in mind that the parents are the primary carers and ultimately need to be given the support to enable them to be 'good enough' parents. Counselling is one important way through which individual parents can be assisted in this way. For example, counselling a depressed mother can indirectly meet the needs of her child. As she begins to understand the roots of her depression and recognises her previous denial of her own needs the woman may become free to respond more appropriately to her child's needs.

Family centres are usually situated in disadvantaged areas with stretched health, social and educational resources. There is often little, if anything, available for people whose problems are not severe enough to reach the psychiatric services unless they can afford to pay for counselling/therapy. Many women may consult their GPs presenting their distress in physical terms. Few GPs, particularly in hard-pressed disadvantaged areas, have time to provide counselling. Many patients, particularly women, are offered anti-depressants which may anaesthetise the pain but do not resolve the original problem. Anti-depressants may be valuable in the short term but counselling can assist the person in obtaining longer-term improvement in their situation.

As already indicated, mothers use family centres far more than fathers. Further to this imbalance, it would appear that it is women who more often seek out, or are referred for, individual counselling within a family centre. Holt (1992) explores some of the issues in engaging men in counselling. Counselling may often be offered to couples and aspects of such work will be considered later in this chapter.

The aims of counselling

Counselling, in common with other methods, has some form of change as its aim. The nature and direction of the change sought will be defined by 'client' and a 'counsellor'. The desired change may be some aspect of the individual or of his/her environment or of the interaction between the two.

Counselling is sought for a variety of difficulties which include depression, anxiety, difficulties in relationships with children or with adults or dealing with violence. It is not rare to find that the current difficulties faced by the parent seeking counselling are significantly caused, or at least compounded by, distressing features in the parent's own childhood such as the experience of physical or sexual abuse, emotional neglect or long periods in care.

A direct or indirect effect of counselling, which may not be associated with the method, is that of empowerment. Counselling can offer adults an opportunity to grow and develop their own potential thus increasing their ability to have control over their circumstances.

Issues of counselling in a family centre

Some of the issues raised by providing counselling in a family centre setting may best be explored by the use of case illustrations.

Example 5.1

Jean is a 24-year-old lone parent with two children, John aged 5 years and Sally aged 3 years. She had a tempestuous and violent relationship with the children's father and has separated from him. Jean's lifestyle tends to be very chaotic and there are constant visitors to her home at all times of day and night. Jean's father was violent towards his wife and children and died when Jean was 10 years old. Nursery staff are concerned about Sally's poor health and delayed development. At a case conference, held after the discovery of a number of bruises on Sally, concerns were expressed about both children and how greatly they were affected by their mother's needs and mood swings. Jean's depression and low self-esteem became very apparent. There was agreement that, unless Jean's own considerable and often childlike needs were responded to, the quality of her parenting skills was unlikely to improve. At the same time, she would also be expected to continue to act as the responsible parent and to work directly on her relationship with the children. The family was consequently referred to the local family centre for (a) individual counselling for Jean and (b) play sessions for Jean and the children in their home with a different family centre worker.

Jean had little trust in helping agencies, and no experience of counselling. She was not used to thinking about herself or having someone else think about her. It was important that counselling was presented to her in a way which made sense to her. Jean rarely left her house so, during the initial stages, the sessions had to take place in

---

her home. At the beginning her ambivalence was demonstrated in a number of ways. These included her being out on several occasions due to 'urgent' appointments or the house being full of friends at the time of the pre-arranged appointment. Jean's difficulty in trusting anyone, which prevented her developing intimate relationships even with her children, was inevitably extended to her relationship with the family centre worker. Thus the worker viewed Jean's 'unavailability' as connected to her difficulties in developing a trusting relationship rather than simply dismissing it as 'resistance' or a refusal to embark on the necessary work. Jean's experience of the worker's persistence and commitment gradually allowed her to take her own needs more seriously.

As indicated, Jean had problems in setting limits and boundaries in her relationships with her children or with other adults. It was important that her worker was able to offer her a different experience, where boundaries and limits were clearly set. To this end sessions were planned well ahead and held at the same time each week. Just dropping in to the house at unarranged times would have added to the feeling of chaos and uncertainty and would have failed to create a safe, secure context in which Jean could begin to explore her feelings. Therefore Jean was always clear about the time, date, place and length of sessions. After some months of often frustrating contact, Jean began to develop a more trusting relationship with the worker so that she could move to the next phase of exploring areas for change. The worker could then begin to negotiate some 'rules', such as no visitors during the hour of their sessions. As Jean developed more self-confidence, she progressed to meeting the worker at the family centre. By this stage she was able to address and express her own needs more clearly and begin to think about her children's needs as separate from her own.

As already discussed, a crucial theme in family centre work is 'who is the client?'. This is particularly pertinent where there are child protection issues. In Example 5.1, where individual counselling was part of the plan, the worker needed to feel free to be present for the mother and not to have the needs of the child as the primary focus. This made it essential for at least one other worker to be allocated to attend to the children. Supervision and discussion with the child-focused worker are also vital ingredients.

As in all contexts for counselling, confidentiality is a vital factor. In Example 5.1 it was important that from the outset there was clear agreement between the parent, family centre and referrer (local social services) about the rules for confidentiality. The adult needs to have trust that the counselling sessions are confidential, yet when child-protection issues arise there may be situations when the information needs to be shared with other agencies. Although this can produce profound difficulties for a counselling relationship, clarification in the earliest stage will greatly reduce the difficulties.

The 'venue' for counselling is often an important question. Using the family centre can assist a parent in focusing on 'the work' free from distraction and interruption. However there may be circumstances, as with Jean, where there are arguments for seeing the individual at home. When this happens the worker needs to find ways of helping the parent to recognise the importance of protecting their session.

Example 5.2 raises other issues of counselling in a family centre.

Example 5.2

Anna is 28 years old, living with her husband Paul and three children, Stephen, 6 years, Amy, 4 years and Jane, 2 years. She was referred to the local family centre by the health visitor who was concerned about Anna's isolation and frequent signs of distress. The health visitor thought that Anna and the children might benefit from attending the centre's 'drop-in' sessions. Initially Anna did not want to be referred for counselling sessions, but was interested in meeting other parents.

Anna brought the two youngest children to the 'drop-in' sessions and attended regularly although she was quiet and shy and had difficulty in joining in group discussion.

She talked 'informally' with staff at the centre and after a few months sought out one of the staff to ask if she could 'talk'. Following an initial discussion with Anna, regular counselling sessions were planned with her.

It became clear that Anna had been feeling depressed since Jane's birth. She felt that Paul did not understand her and did not help to care for the children. She was disappointed that her mother had irregular contact with her and thought that her sisters received greater maternal support. Her mother had remarried when Anna was 9 years old, Anna never got on with her stepfather and mourned the loss of her father who had left the family three years before her mother's remarriage. Anna used counselling to explore and express feelings of loss and rejection and to identify the nature of the relationships she desired with her mother and sister. She gained the confidence to renegotiate these relationships.

In exploring her relationship with Paul, Anna and the worker identified the need for joint work with Paul. Subsequently a male member of staff was able to do some time-limited work with the original worker and the couple.

Anna's gain in self-esteem and confidence was demonstrated by her increasing contribution to other activities at the family centre, such as playing a welcoming role to newcomers at the 'drop-in' sessions and joining with other parents and staff to organise events. Thus she was encouraged to have a holistic view of herself as a person with strengths as well as vulnerabilities and had opportunities both to give and to receive.

The open-door policy of the family centre allowed Anna the opportunity to familiarise herself with the centre and staff and to feel comfortable in the surroundings before asking for counselling. In this way she was able to come to it in her own time and could exercise some elements of control in choosing the staff member to whom she related best.

However, counselling in such a setting is not without its dilemmas and constraints. Moving between the different roles involved in an informal 'drop-in' and more 'formal' counselling can be stressful for both parents and staff. At times Anna had difficulty in managing the subtle changes in the relationship with the worker between the 'drop-in' session, counselling sessions and committee meetings. Although the situation felt difficult at times, the worker was able to use these experiences constructively to help Anna to explore openly feelings of rejection and problems in sharing attention.

Parents who attended Fulford Family Centre (1991), talking of the benefits of counselling, said:

> I realise now what a wonderful service it was . . . it's made me understand myself a lot better. They sort of nursed me along to be able to talk, being encouraged is an important part.

> I've got a completely different attitude now. I used to do things without thinking about it. I used to walk straight into trouble. I'm not so quick-tempered any more, not so quick-tempered with the children. We have more good times together now.

Transactional analysis

One particular approach which has obvious relevance to family centres and is therefore selected for specific, though brief, mention is that of *transactional analysis*. This can be illuminating in understanding some of the confusing communications and interactions which take place within a family centre. Berne (1966) the originator of transactional analysis identifies three primary ego states, which can be viewed as parts of the personality and which involve both feelings and behaviour:

Parent behaviour based on values and attitudes and represented by nurture or criticism.

Adult behaviour characterised by thinking and deciding.

Child expresses a person's emotional response to a situation.

Behaviour can be identified as originating from one of these three states, as in Example 5.3.

Example 5.3

Parent of 3-year-old James to member of staff, 'The Smith family should be banned from the centre because Peter hit James and the Smiths don't discipline Peter like they should.' (*parent state*)

'I'm wondering if James has got an ear infection.' (*adult state*)

'I'm going to give up coming to the centre, you never seem to have time for me, that new family is obviously more important.' (*child state*)

In the above examples, and in any interaction, staff may also respond from one of the three ego states. It can be helpful to recognise which state a parent is 'coming from' in order to respond most effectively. Apart from its value as a therapeutic method, transactional analysis provides a model to understand why communication is going wrong and parents and/or staff are feeling confused or misunderstood. It is also a tool which can be shared fairly readily with parents and thus used together. There is not the opportunity to provide further detail of transactional analysis here as it is a comprehensive framework. However a number of sources such as Pitman (1984) and (1990) and James and Jongeward (1971) giving a fuller account are available and are worth exploring.

Working with couples and families

As with counselling or individual therapy, family therapy also demonstrates numerous models. Some details of different family therapy approaches and issues surrounding their application are found in Street and Dryden (1988). Many of the issues raised in looking at work with individuals also apply to working with couples and families and so will not be repeated here.

Work with a couple or family is likely to be an appropriate approach when it is apparent that change is required within the family's patterns of interaction. There are fundamental questions about who is to be seen within a family and how they are to be engaged. Family centres can often offer flexible and creative answers to such questions. The entry to family work will vary and, where work starts with one individual, careful thought must be given to how other family members will 'join'. In a family centre where work is mainly with older children or adolescents the young person may be the initial 'client'. Where it then seems appropriate to include the rest of the family considerable preparation may be needed both of the young person and of his/her family.

In centres mainly concerned with young children and their families, work with the adult couple is more likely than whole family sessions. However, it may be useful to have some sessions where the children are present, as they can provide useful information about the parent/child relationships. Young children who have not yet fully developed their verbal communication may not be able to participate in the therapeutic 'dialogue' but their behaviour may provide illuminating data about the family dynamics. Thus their involvement may be most relevant in the assessment stages of the work with the family. When the work moves into more of a 'treatment' mode (this is not to deny that assessment and reassessment are continuing processes) it may be appropriate to work with just the parents. Despite this, as explored in a later chapter, play sessions with the whole family may be an appropriate therapeutic approach and a useful therapy model for work with parents and young children.

An additional question to that of which family members are to be involved in family sessions, is who is to undertake the work. Work with a couple or family is likely to be facilitated by co-work. Where one family member has already been engaged in work with the centre, the introduction of a co-worker who plays a primary role in engaging the previously absent family members may be particularly useful. A combination of paired individual work and co-work with the couple can be fruitful.

Example 5.4

In Example 5.2 after the need for marital work was identified through counselling with Anna, another worker established individual sessions with Paul as one stage of a plan (agreed with both Anna and Paul) to undertake joint work with the couple. After the other worker's individual sessions with Paul, both workers met for a series of sessions with the couple.

The involvement of another worker when engaging additional family members can help to prevent the 'new' members feeling that the worker is already allied to one family member and therefore unlikely to understand their position in the family.

Groupwork in a family centre

Who are groups for?

The nature of groupwork and the types of group involved will depend on the model of family centre. Thus a referral-based, or 'client-focused' family centre is likely to run therapy-based closed groups for parents/families, whereas a neighbourhood-based family centre, with a high level of self-referrals and emphasis on user participation, is likely to run a wider variety of groups, with demands from users contributing to decisions about the group programme. Thus, planning groups within the latter model of centre involves negotiation between users and staff and possibly outside agencies. Negotiation whose outcome is acceptable to all parties will depend on a shared understanding and definition of priorities. It is perhaps inevitable that there will be times when parents' desire for further groups to repeat previous good experiences may be denied by a priority to meet hitherto unmet need. Similarly, individual staff preference for a particular type of group may be denied by the requirement to meet the demands of another agency.

Example 5.5

Few black families lived in the neighbourhood of Fulford Family Centre and those that did frequently experienced racism. Only one or two black families used the centre but, learning of their experiences, staff proposed a group for parents of black children as a priority for the centre. The proposal was put to the Parents' Council and the initial response was one of hesitancy. The parents on the council, none of whom had black children, identified other groups which they thought were more important and argued that 'no one is stopping black families coming to things that already happen at the centre'. After several debates and discussions, the staff and parents jointly agreed that a group for the parents of black children should be a priority.

A range of groups

In common with other day or residential establishments, work in family centres frequently involves what Brown and Clough (1989, p. 21) have defined as a 'complex mosaic of groups and groupings'. The specific groups and groupings will vary in terms of their aims, focus, membership, worker role, relationship with other groups/groupings, and their developmental stage.

A number of issues are connected with the concept of membership. Thus there are questions of entry criteria which decide who has access to a centre and its groups. Different groups within a centre may have different entry criteria. Entry criteria raise issues of exclusion and inclusion.

Example 5.6

A group for lone parents at Fulford, initially very 'successful', foundered when other parents not recognisably 'lone' but defining themselves as such in terms of sole responsibility for their children, resented the group's

> entry criteria and insisted that they should be included in the group.

Whether groups have an open or closed membership is also a distinguishing aspect of different groups. Many family centres will employ a range of closed and open groups. Closed groups have a fixed membership and are usually time-limited. In contrast, open groups are often open in both terms of membership and the life span of the group.

Group membership also needs to be considered in terms of group composition. Brown (1986, p. 37) suggests that the 'key decisions in group composition are concerned with homogeneity and heterogeneity, balance and compatibility'. Often, within the context of a family centre, potential group-members are already known to staff and thus considerable knowledge is already possessed about common attributes and different behaviours. This can assist the workers in making informed decisions about compatibility and balance and in identifying, for instance, key informal 'leaders' whose participation in a group will encourage and motivate others.

Groups common to family centres

A selection of groups likely to be found associated with family centres will be explored here.

1 Parents'/parenting groups
These are likely to be a feature of many family centres. Questions that need addressing include:

(a) *Membership* – are potential members referred by other agencies, recruited from existing centre participants, obtained by external advertisement or a mixture of all three?
(b) *Dangers of stigmatisation* – is the group for any parent or is it defined or viewed as a group for 'bad' parents or for parents whose children are looked after by the local authority?
(c) *Aims of the group* – are they educational or therapeutic? This will also influence the two previous questions.

(d) *Position in the local welfare services network* – will the group contribute to assessment under the Children Act? If families are referred by social workers how will those workers be involved?

(e) *'Follow-on' for members* – how can families be helped to 'move on'? The group may involve members with considerable emotional needs who, benefiting from the group and workers' nurturing, may be unable/unwilling to progress into less intensively nurturing groups within the time span required by the group/centre.

(f) *'Parents or mothers'* – how can a centre ensure that, where relevant, fathers are engaged? The conviction, communicated to both families and referrers, that the father in a household must be involved in parenting groups in order for change to occur may be an essential starting-point.

2 Personal development/issue groups

Such groups focus less on parenting and more on issues for individual members. They may encompass, for example, women's groups, health groups, assertiveness training. They may bring together individuals with common experiences or difficulties such as a prisoners' wives group or a group for survivors of sexual abuse. Pertinent issues include:

(a) *Parents as individuals* – these groups embody the 'holistic' ideals of many family centres by attending to the 'whole' person and their needs and not just seeing adult users as 'parents'. A women's group can enable its members to identify the pressure from expectations placed on them as 'mothers'. Members can support each other in discovering their individual potential and their collective concerns. The group can promote individual growth and development.

(b) *Recruitment* – these groups often arise from existing centre participants' expressed need and interests and therefore there is a prepared constituency for recruitment.

(c) *Familiarity* – following on from the above issue, most of the eventual group members are likely to know each other already from other groups/groupings in the centre. This can result in inappropriate importing of cultures, roles and norms from other groups. This will be explored further later in this section.

3 Informal groups

Neighbourhood family centres often encourage the development of informal groups. These are usually open groups and may aim to attract as wide a spectrum of users as possible. Such groups may be run along the lines of parent and toddler or 'drop-in' groups and may meet a number of objectives. Crucial questions for such groups which need to be addressed include:

● Who sets the agenda/establishes ground-rules?
● How are such groups staffed and what are the staff roles?
● How are outsiders/newcomers treated?
● How are unwelcoming cliques avoided?
● What decision-making powers does the group have and how are decisions communicated?
● How are power differentials addressed?
● Who is responsible for the children and their activities?

4 Self-help groups

Family centres can offer unique resources for facilitating self-help groups. These resources include the physical facilities such as a venue, equipment, secretarial provision. In addition access may be provided to human resources such as the ability to tap into local informal and formal networks, or the provision of staff expertise or facilitation. The relationships between a family centre and self-help groups require thoughtful attention. The issues involved are explored by Adams (1990) and his identification of aspects of the social worker's role in facilitating self-help are highly relevant to family centres. He writes that the role of the social worker may be summarised as follows:

1. Establishing at the outset a boundary rather than a central role for the social worker.

2. Not taking the lead in determining the focus, the pace of activity, the goals or the means of getting there.
3. Standing alongside the self-helpers rather than above them in terms of power, skills and professional activity.
4. Acting as someone who is available to be consulted rather than as an imposed, supervisory presence.

(Adams, 1990, p. 51)

The context for groupwork

The advantages of working with groups as a method or a target of intervention have been described many times and do not need rehearsing here (Brown, 1986; Douglas, 1976, 1978 and 1983; McCaughan, 1978; Preston-Shoot, 1987). However the wider context of the family centre needs to be examined.

There may be issues in maintaining a groupwork programme. In a period when social services' resources are not expanding at the same rate as the demands made on them, many family centres will experience increased demands on them for work with individuals and families, of a nature previously carried out by social services departments' area teams. This can lead to the danger of increasing individual or family work at the expense of groupwork. Action which can help in maintaining a groupwork programme includes:

(a) ensuring that a groupwork programme is devised when a centre is first established;
(b) listening to participants – they will keep asking for groups;
(c) evaluating each group and ensuring that the effectiveness of every group is publicised;
(d) allocating responsibility to one or more members of staff for co-ordinating groupwork.

As identified by Stones (1989), a central issue for groups in a family centre is the concurrent membership by both staff and families of several groups and groupings. For staff and users, advantages of the varied relationships and settings they experience together can be the reassurance of familiarity and more readily established confidence and trust. But there can be disadvantages, as indicated earlier, such as the transfer of inappropriate norms. The importing of the norms of an open, informal group into a closed group focusing on distressing personal issues is likely to detract seriously from the creation of a safe and secure group culture. Strategies to combat these risks include the use of structured beginning and ending exercises and the establishment of specific ground-rules for every new group, which acknowledge differences from other groups.

Group-members can find themselves constrained to one particular role by other group experiences. Thus a family centre participant may be expected to play the role of 'jester' whatever group she attends. Staff need to be careful not to impose existing perceptions of participants onto their membership of every group, for example, relying on and encouraging 'competent' members always to help with group maintenance tasks.

The openness of many family centres also carries benefits and dangers. Stigma may be overcome but privacy threatened. Publicity in an open family centre about the group programme can lead to awareness amongst participants about 'who does what'.

Example 5.7

At Fulford when a group was arranged for survivors of sexual abuse, some participants worried that, 'everyone will know where I am going and so they'll guess what happened to me'.

Much has been written in groupwork literature about leadership in groups and the role of the workers. Most groups and workers benefit from co-leadership and this requires open and honest communication between the workers concerned.

The mosaic of groups and groupings inevitably leads to inter-group relationships. These can be collaborative or competitive. The establishment of a 'new' group without prior discussion and negotiation with existing groups and members can be fatal for the potential group. Workers may sometimes underestimate the amount of preparation of existing participants which is required.

Example 5.8

A group initiated for 'newcomers' which included insufficient preparation of current centre-users was in danger of sabotage by them. The establishment of the newcomers' group required, for a period of time, a reduction of staff presence in an existing informal group. Staff were surprised by the degree of resentment from the informal group members who expressed feelings of betrayal and neglect by 'their' staff.

Working with groups in a family-centre setting means that considerable attention needs to be paid to the wider context. No group can be considered as an isolated entity; each is enmeshed in a fascinating matrix of individuals, groups and groupings.

Groups are a central approach in many family centres and valued by users as the following comments from group members indicate:

> Parents currently working within a group together spoke of the trust and friendship they share with fellow-members. They are able to give each other support and feel it is good to be with other people who understand their struggles.
>
> One parent valued groups where she had been able to learn parenting skills or share particular experiences with other parents. 'I didn't use to like groups of people, I found them scary but they're alright now. I realise what I have to say isn't worthless for it can help somebody else.' (Fulford Family Centre, 1991).

Community work from a family centre base

The degree and nature of a family centre's interaction with its local neighbourhood depends to a great extent on the type of centre and its location. Where the neighbourhood context for families is given serious consideration this aspect of a centre's approach may be variously defined as 'community work', 'community development', 'community social work', 'neighbourhood work' or a 'community orientation'. The different semantics are confusing and it is frequently unclear whether different words are being used to describe the same activity or the same words are being used by different people to describe discrete activities. For the purposes of this chapter, we will use the term 'community work'. The objectives of community work are usually concerned with bringing about change in the environment and also with enabling local people both to define and to express community needs. There is also an attendant aim of encouraging the development of the skills and resources within the local community. The means of achieving these aims always emphasises the importance of collective action. Twelvetrees (1982) explores the principles and practice of community work.

Why community work in a family centre?

The problems and opportunities which face families are not confined to the characteristics and relationships found within the family. Environmental and structural factors play a highly significant role in the quality of family life. A family centre can address some of these factors through a community-work approach. A second reason for the use of a community work perspective is that it encourages the forging of links between formal and informal networks. The services which families receive are often compartmentalised and fragmented. There is rarely help in connecting the fragments or identifying and filling 'the gaps'.

In exploring community work, a first and vital question is which community? A first assumption usually associates community with a geographical location and hence the occasional practice of equating community work and neighbourhood work. However, it is also recognised that other kinds of community exist which are usually described as 'communities-of-interest'. These, as the phrase suggests, are groups or networks sharing a common interest and often unrelated to geographical location. For a family centre both types of community may be of relevance. Thus a centre will be concerned with the immediate geographical neighbourhood and its community networks and groups. The nature of the centre's remit may also mean that its particular focus will be a community of interest relating to young families or adolescents and their families. These two types of communities may be combined so that a centre will focus on the 'community of young families' within the specific neighbourhood.

Know your community

Any family centre embarking on community work needs to know its community. A systematic way in which this can be begun is by producing a community profile. This provides a picture of the community including its strengths and weaknesses. Sources of information for a profile include:

- public reports and statistics such as census data;
- local authority reports;
- information from local residents;
- information from locally based agencies such as health centres and churches (Henderson and Thomas, 1989).

In producing a profile a family centre will gain information about the following issues:

1. *Physical boundaries* For young families their neighbourhood, and thus a family centre's immediate neighbourhood, is 'pram-pushing' or 'toddler-walking' distance. Some geographical communities are assisted by clear physical boundaries; other neighbourhoods may be difficult to delineate due to a continuous residential/rural area without obvious boundaries.
2. *Hidden divisions* These result from various factors:
Physical features such as open spaces, major roads or nonresidential areas.
The nature of housing provision, such as the size of units, influences the demographic structure of the com-

munity. Thus a preponderance of one type of housing can lead to a concentration of families with a particular age of children.

The commitment of residents to the neighbourhood will be affected by the length of time they have lived there and the degree of choice leading to their residence. Recognised disadvantaged neighbourhoods, not surprisingly, frequently contain residents whose primary aim is to obtain rehousing and leave the area. Residents living in stressful circumstances may have little free energy to become involved in community activity.

3. *Resourceful residents* A community may contain well-established residents who are a stabilising and regenerative force. There may be individuals who have time and energy to invest outside their home and/or work, to be involved in community groups, etc. Such individuals may also be in the position to offer informal support and practical help to more stressed families.

4. *Ethnicity* A family centre needs to know both the ethnic composition of the neighbourhood and the issues surrounding ethnicity in the locality. The position in the community of members of minority ethnic groups may be well-established and secure, or vulnerable and isolated. Different neighbourhoods demonstrate different degrees and different forms of racism.

5. *Community balance* A balanced community contains a mixture of ages, maturity, skills, family and financial circumstances, nature of home tenure and degrees of stress. A wide discrepancy from the national 'norm' in any factor can create an unbalanced community. There is a considerable difference in the implications between a national average, for example, of 14 per cent lone parent families and a local community composition of 40 per cent.

6. *Accessibility or isolation of the community* can greatly influence its strengths. This interacts with the balance of the community. Thus a balanced community may not be affected by isolation, having access within itself to a breadth of skills and resources. In contrast, an 'unbalanced' community may need to 'import' skills from adjoining areas and isolation will militate against this.

Roles and relationships in community work

As Henderson and Thomas (1989, p. 103) point out there is 'a proliferation of labels in community work literature that describe the roles open to the worker'. Community work from a family centre base requires the workers concerned to move easily between a number of roles and relationships. For the purposes of this chapter only certain aspects can be explored. Certain relevant roles are outlined below.

Facilitator A worker may enable individual community groups to work more effectively and also increase their power and influence by bringing together fragmented small groups into a larger body.

Example 5.9

A family-centre development worker facilitated an existing parent/toddler group which needed to find a new venue and was stagnating. As a result the group moved to new premises and began to recruit new members.

Example 5.10

The development worker brought together a number of parent/toddler groups to be a more powerful lobby for safe play opportunities for young children in the area.

Fact gatherer, analyst and publicist These vital roles can be played in researching and drawing together information about a particular community need. The resultant findings may then need publicising to draw necessary resources to the community.

Example 5.11

Fulford Family Centre used census data to identify the location of families with under-fives. To their surprise they discovered a concentration of young families in multi-storey blocks of flats. A survey was undertaken to discover precise numbers and the problems encountered by families with children under five in high-rise flats. The published findings led, amongst other things, to the local authority reconsidering aspects of its housing policy and the establishment of a 'high-rise' working party. The centre was subsequently successful in obtaining time-limited central government funding to employ a 'high-rise' resource worker.

Network encourager   Networks play an essential part in a family's quality of life. Paucity in the nature or extent of a family's network may be the result of a number of factors. These cover the constraints placed on a parent by caring for young children, a neighbourhood lacking formal and informal groups to join, a high rate of burglaries or vandalism which discourages families from leaving their homes unattended, to lack of confidence or social skills possessed by the parent.

Example 5.12

One of the aims of the 'high-rise' resource worker, referred to in the previous example, was to provide an opportunity for families to build up networks and thus counteract the isolation many of them were experiencing. A parent-and-toddler group was set up on each of the high-rise sites. Each group, initially composed of strangers, saw the development of arrangements for mutual child-minding, outings and informal meetings in members' homes.

Catalyst   A central community-work role is working with residents to assist in identifying gaps and promoting developments to fill them.

Example 5.13

The effect of 'loan sharks' on local families in poverty was very apparent to the family centre. Parents talked of being unable to prepare for Christmas as they were still paying off loans at exorbitant rates from the previous Christmas. A worker brought together some local parents and together they explored the possibilities and requirements of establishing a Credit Union.

Encourager   Obtaining changes and improvements in a neighbourhood can be a long, slow and frustrating process. Residents daily experiencing disadvantage and environmental deprivation may, understandably, become disheartened and discouraged by the lack of immediate change. Workers with experience of the complex processes of public authorities and with a breadth of vision of possibilities and potential may be required to provide encouragement.

Example 5.14

The 'high-rise' groups identified the need for a safe external play area as a high priority. Encouraged by the worker and nurtured by their groups some residents attended the High-Rise Working Party and others became active in the tenants' association. The local Housing Department acknowledged the need identified by the parents and outlined plans for a play area/ community garden. In the subsequent long period, mainly related to waiting for available finance, residents expressed discouragement and doubt as to whether their hopes would ever be realised. The worker provided support and enabled the group to obtain feedback from the Housing Department about progress and causes of delay.

Broker   Local families may need assistance in being put in touch with policy-makers and resource-holders. Likewise, and sometimes more surprisingly, public bodies need forums to consult local residents. Family centres may play a fundamental role in enabling the different 'parties' to gain access to each other. Public bodies, whilst emphasising the importance of consultation, are sometimes ambivalent (and often unskilled) about providing it. Family centres involved in community work may play a vital role in ensuring that consultation is genuine and that residents are appropriately equipped – for example, with the necessary information – to participate in consultation.

Example 5.15

A local planning officer asked the family centre to assist in obtaining the views of residents in a small development of council flats about a proposal to plant trees in their communal green. Users of the centre, living in the development, undertook a survey of their neighbours' views which demonstrated a large majority against the proposal. When the results were conveyed to the planning officer he shamefacedly revealed that the trees had already been purchased! They were consequently planted elsewhere.

Educator/trainer Parents in contact with a family centre may lack skills and confidence. A family centre's involvement in community development can provide opportunities for its users to develop skills and gain confidence. Often the mothers involved in a centre have had unsatisfying educational experience and have noticeably underachieved. Their – often early – involvement in child-bearing and child-rearing has compounded their lack of opportunities. Centres committed to the development of leadership skills within the community need to recognise that there may be a cycle of training and 'losing' leaders. Parents who gain in skills and confidence will wish to apply their skills appropriately in obtaining paid employment or pursuing further interests or training. Such activities may result in the removal of their energy and skills from the local neighbourhood.

Communicator Involvement in community work may require workers to work with groups containing both residents and workers. Such groups may need to work hard at effective communication. Professional workers can easily lapse into shorthand jargon leaving local residents feeling excluded. Workers through training and experience may be very familiar with procedures, rules and structures and residents may be hesitant to show their 'ignorance' by seeking clarification.

Campaigns or consultation may not produce the results which residents or professionals desired. Plans may fail because of lack of funding or unforeseen budget cuts. In these circumstances, residents are likely to feel alienated and deeply disappointed. Workers will often share the disappointment, which needs to be acknowledged if it is not to lead to residents demonstrating apathy and a reluctance to continue involvement because of the lack of results. Similarly 'successes', however small, need to be recognised and publicised so that they can be built upon.

One parent from Fulford (1991) commenting on the encouragement she had found from being involved in the local neighbourhood said:

> I've learnt the value of group action; forming groups with a neighbourhood can make changes happen.

Working with the local community and other agencies can place family centre workers in conflict with their own or other organisations (Phelan, 1983). Campaigns and protests about lack of resources for children and parents are rarely welcomed by the resource providers yet they do not inevitably lead to destructive conflict or impasse. Family centres are often well-placed to encourage the conflict between members of the neighbourhood and public authorities over insufficient or badly managed resources to develop into something creative and productive.

6

A Child Perspective

The importance of a child perspective

Wordsworth's assertion, 'the child is father of the man,' is an often-quoted insight into the powerful formative influence of childhood. Psychological theories provide an understanding of some of the processes through which the experiences of childhood, interacting with the child's innate potential, can affect the individual throughout their life. The development of young humans from birth results in them being dependent on adults for a considerable length of time. Yet, in spite of knowledge about children's needs, society's attitude to children appears ambiguous. There is a United Nations' Charter asserting the basic rights of children, but throughout the world children continue to be exploited. In Britain various legislation, most recently the Children Act 1989, propagates the rights of children and indicates the responsibilities of parents and of public authorities. Yet there is also a public neglect of children's needs. Examples of this are the numbers of children in bed-and-breakfast accommodation; the problem of access to public buildings and public transport for prams and 'buggies'; and the lack of any comprehensive provision of playgroups or nursery places.

A child perspective, whether at a 'macro' level of social policy and welfare planning or at a 'micro' level of the work of an individual family centre, requires that the needs of children are recognised and addressed. Children have a range of inter-related needs which must be met to a 'good-enough' degree if they are to grow into healthy and mature adults. Their needs vary at different developmental stages and between individual children. This text cannot go into a detailed account of child development. There are many other sources for such detail; but it is relevant to make a few pertinent comments.

It is sometimes assumed in an affluent society with decreased infant mortality rates that children's physical needs are being met readily. However many families in contact with family centres are reliant on public benefits as their main source of income. The comparatively low level of such income can result in families facing extreme difficulties in providing adequate nutrition for their children. In addition to the basic need for food and drink, a child's physical needs also include rest, exercise and safety. Children with a disability or learning difficulties may have additional physical needs.

The healthy psychological development of a child relies on, amongst other vital elements, the evolution of a coherent identity and a positive self-image. To foster these, issues of race and gender need to be acknowledged. Sexism and personal and institutional racism may result in stereotypes, with detrimental effect on a child's self-image.

Play has a central role in both the social and intellectual development of children. Unfortunately the essential nature of play is still not widely recognised. It is denigrated with, for example, 'child's play' being used as a synonym for something trivial and unimportant.

Bowlby (1979, 1980) and others' theories on the infant's attachment to its mother (or primary care-giver) provide valuable insights into the role which such bonding plays in the foundation of a child's psychological, physical and cognitive development. Unfortunately there has been a tendency for such insights to be used to pressurise parents (usually mothers) to carry sole responsibility for meeting their children's needs. Often insufficient attention has been paid to the support and resources parents need to fulfil their demanding responsibilities. As noted earlier, the Children Act's notion of partnership between parents and public authorities is an important concept which moves from the unhelpful 'either/or' of much provision for children.

Services for children suffer from being the responsibility of several authorities. A child's health, education, day care and leisure activities are each the concern of different departments and agencies. Services vary in their underlying principles and philosophy (Pugh, 1988). Varied provision involves staff with different training and qualification. Much work with young children is poorly paid and carries low status. Yet, as indicated, there is much evidence that the earliest years are some of the most formative in a person's life. Some areas have made noteworthy attempts to coordinate provision for under-fives and thus provide a more coherent and consistent programme.

Implications of a child perspective

The implications of a child perspective permeate all aspects of a family centre: from the building to its staffing, from the equipment to the programme. It is surprising how often the needs of children are overlooked in the design and adaptation of public buildings and family centres themselves do not always escape this oversight. It is essential that architects and planners consult people with knowledge and experience of working with children before designing family centre buildings. It is important not only to take into account the general needs of children and the special needs of children with disabilities but also any particular local features. In an area where the majority of families live in flats lacking both inner and outer play spaces, a centre may need to allocate extensive space to encourage physical play. In an inner city area with few green spaces then using some outside space as a garden will be essential.

Clearly, a child perspective, and one appropriate to the age of the children using the centre, is vital in selecting equipment and materials. These need to be suited both to the developmental needs of the children and, in many centres, to heavy use by numbers of children. All centres need to choose materials which are representative of a multi-ethnic society and avoid stereotypes of race, gender, or family composition. Browne and France (1986) indicate how many preschool posters and pictures present racist and/or sexist images. Purchasing appropriate materials requires the dedication of sufficient financial resources to children's needs.

The design, furnishing and equipping of a centre have considerable influence on whether a family centre is felt to be a place where children are welcomed and valued. Wherever possible, children themselves should be involved in choices and decisions about the physical environment.

A child perspective should also influence the design and content of a centre's programme. In centres where much of the work is focused on parents and parenting, the long-term needs of the children may be being well-served but their immediate needs may be inadvertently neglected. Careful attention may have been paid to the planning and setting up of a parents' group with little thought given to the parallel children's group. This may be symbolised by it being called a crèche and only scant consideration being given to the particular configuration of children, their individual developmental needs and the likely interaction between the children.

As explored in an earlier chapter, family centres have an important role to play as advocates for children's needs. This advocacy will sometimes be addressed towards parents who are individually or collectively failing to perceive or respond to the child(ren)'s needs. A simple example is parents' objections to painting or 'messy' play. Family centre staff (often with the support of other parents) may need to explain the importance of such activities.

Staff are a crucial factor in a centre's quality of provision for children. As Wood *el al.* (1980, pp. 192–3) point out in their studies of practitioners working with under-fives:

> But particularly in conversation, play and instruction, we found that the competence displayed by the young rested on the adult's style of working . . . The adult is a primary ingredient in pre-school care, the major resource.

Working with individual children

Much of a family centre's work with children will probably be spent either with groups of children or with parents and children together. But there will also be occasions when the needs of an individual child and/or family requires work with a child on his/her own. There are many different tools for assessing the needs of individual children and centres vary as to how systematic or rigorous they are in observing and assessing children.

The use of developmental guides in assessing children over a period of time enables staff and parents to recognise progress and identify specific problems or developmental delay. Many different developmental guides and assessment charts are available, for example, National Children's Bureau, Portage, or Sheridan, but they all tend to cover common areas. If a centre wants to keep structured records on individual children, then a number of factors are relevant in selecting the most appropriate charts to use. Thought should be given to how any assessment can be carried out jointly with parents and to this end any chart or form needs to be readily understood and easily used. In work with individual children it is usually important to collaborate with other agencies concerned with the child and his/her family so consideration might be given to different local professionals using identical or readily compatible developmental records.

In any assessment it is important to recognise and emphasise that each child should be seen as an individual and their progress appraised within their singular context. For 'although all children must accomplish the same developmental tasks, each individual child approaches them in a way that reflects his unique predispositions and experiences' (Fahlberg, 1982, p. 5). Clearly, there will be some awareness of developmental norms but this should form a backdrop rather than a focus for any assessment. Most guides encourage this attitude by taking a developmental rather than an 'ages and stages' approach, as the latter approach can lead to parents becoming disheartened and over anxious over their child 'failing'.

Work with an individual child may arise from the concern of a parent, centre staff or another agency. The nature of the work will depend on the identified need and resultant aim of intervention. In some instances, a child may benefit from some individual sessions because his/her unfamiliarity with play materials and the company of other children makes it very difficult for the child to participate in group sessions.

Individual sessions with a member of staff may help a child to tolerate periods of separation from his/her parent where this is proving difficult to manage.

Individual play sessions may also assist a child in comprehending or assimilating difficult events. For example, some of the emotional effects of an unexpected hospital admission may be resolved through a child spending several sessions 'playing hospitals'.

Staff in some family centres may possess the skills and experience to offer play therapy to children. Such intervention can provide the opportunity for a child to communicate his/her distress to an understanding adult and with the help of the adult to make sense of perplexing feelings or experiences. The work with the child will also help to assimilate and integrate experiences which have been too painful or difficult for a young child to incorporate unaided. For example, family centres are often in contact with families where children may be experiencing unplanned periods in local authority care or accommodation. This can lead to confusion and distress for the child but a safe and familiar environment where the experiences can be worked through in play may reduce the negative impact of such events.

Example 6.1

Five-year-old Anna appeared to be a confused and anxious child. Her behaviour was sometimes clinging and on other occasions angry and rejecting towards her mother and towards staff. She was frequently punished by her mother for her spiteful behaviour towards her younger brother. After some contact with the centre, her mother revealed that Anna had spent several unplanned periods with foster-parents. Through play sessions with an experienced member of staff Anna eventually felt safe enough to express and explore her varied and powerful feelings relating to the disruptions in her life. The families in the dolls' house allowed her to communicate her ambivalence towards her mother and younger brother, who had remained at home.

In common with its adult equivalent of counselling or therapy, play therapy requires expertise. Whilst words as a medium for communication provide some opportunities for misunderstanding and misinterpretation, a single drawing or action in play can symbolise numerous different feelings or events.

In establishing play-therapy sessions it is important that attention is paid to various factors. Obviously there is a need to prepare the parent(s) prior to commencing work with a child. Individual sessions with a child can be easily sabotaged or unhelpfully influenced by an ill-prepared parent. Parents also need to understand that a child may demonstrate behaviour that they find difficult after sessions. It may be important to establish a contract with the parent about the play sessions. Often a child who is in some distress and in need of play therapy has a parent who is also distressed or in difficulty so it is important that the parents' needs are also being addressed by other staff whilst the child is receiving help. As with most methods of intervention in a family centre, thought needs to be given to the wider context in which the work is being undertaken. Thus, whilst traditional play therapy is undertaken in a setting where child and therapist only meet for contracted sessions, a family centre is likely to involve varied contacts between child and 'therapist'; probably including the child observing 'their' worker with other children. The powerful feelings of envy and resentment that this may provoke need to be acknowledged with the child.

A worker embarking on play-therapy sessions with a child needs to ensure that the time, space and materials are protected and consistent. It is most useful if the child has his/her own 'special box' which is available at each session and contains appropriate materials. It is important to provide suitable support and skilled supervision for staff engaged in play therapy. McMahon (1992) provides a comprehensive introduction to play therapy.

Working with groups of children

Working with groups of children may form a major part of a centre's programme. Depending on their type, many family centres will need to be registered with their local authority under the Children Act 1989. Such registration imposes various requirements on the centre and advice is provided as to appropriate standards in volume 2 of the Children Act guidance and regulations.

Many centres may be engaged in providing day care for children whilst others may have nursery classes attached. In some centres sessions of day care or education may be provided without the presence of parents. In others, parents will be present for much of the time and in yet others there may be both periods of parental involvement and periods of separation of children from parents.

Groupwork with children may pursue a variety of aims, such as providing children with opportunities for socialisation, or developing cooperative play. Groups may be formed of children with common or similar needs; for example, centres may work with a group of children from lone-parent families or a group of children who are black or of mixed parentage. Clarity is needed in thinking about the aims of work with groups of children and the appropriate means of achieving these aims. Taking as an example working with a group of black children, appropriate aims for such a group, almost regardless of the age of the children, may include increasing black-self-awareness and pride, and developing skills to combat the effect of racism. The ways of meeting the aims with young children will obviously focus on play, with some discussion and utilisation of age-appropriate stories, posters, music and videos. Such a group would clearly be most effective if run by a black worker.

The purpose of the group will affect whether it is an open or closed group and, as discussed earlier, if the group is associated with a parallel group for parents then the latter may be very influential in decisions about the children's group. Thus the adult members of a lone-parents' group may wish to open the group to new members at a stage when the associated children's group has not yet developed feelings of stability and security for its members.

Various resources need to be committed to work with groups of children. The physical setting too needs to be suitable for the purpose and nature of the group. Thus a group which is to engage in physical activity should have adequate space to encourage this. If a group includes story-telling/ reading or discussion the space needs to be sufficiently small or enclosed to retain attention and allow everyone to hear and be heard. Often a single space has to be utilised for different activities and different groups, and imagination is needed to divide the space.

Family centres may run activities in venues where they do not own or have sole control over the space. The preparation and clearing-up involved in the use of other venues should never be under-estimated.

When considering materials and equipment for groupwork with children they need to be both child- and worker-'friendly'. Moving and storing equipment can be very demanding physically and this should be borne in mind when selecting resources. Comments made earlier about materials providing anti-racist and anti-sexist perspectives apply here, as in all aspects of family-centre work.

Certain issues relating to staff resources are considered elsewhere in this book, so here it is only necessary to highlight aspects particularly related to working with groups of children. Some groups clearly require constancy in the staff allocated to the group. In other circumstances, although constancy would be ideal, the work with the children may be shared by a group of adults. Communication between staff of observations regarding the progress or needs of individual children will be imperative in such situations. The number of staff required depends on the age and needs of the children. With a wide age-range of children it can be difficult to ensure that individual needs are met so more staff resources may be required. Too high a ratio of children to adults results in the adults spending a large proportion of their time in 'supervisory' or 'management' activities rather than being able to engage in vital interactions with individual children.

Example 6.2

Fulford established a whole-day programme for families where agencies, and sometimes parents themselves, held serious concerns about the standard of child care. Part of the day involved parents and children meeting in separate groups. The children's group could not be composed optimally as membership mainly rested on the parents' need for referral. This sometimes led to a disparate group of children making complex demands on staff and space: three infants, all under 1-year-old, needed protected space to lie or sit on the floor with various appropriate toys; 4-year-old Matthew and 3-year-old Shaun, both highly active children, needed considerable physical space and demanded a lot of interaction with staff; Sarah, aged 2, was a quiet, withdrawn child who could all too easily be overlooked; 4-year-old Simon had speech difficulties and his frustration at often being misunderstood led to fierce temper tantrums. Each session of the children's group had to be carefully planned to ensure that the space and staff resources were used most appropriately to meet the children's needs.

When working with groups of children it is important that family centres set and meet appropriate standards for such work. This not only ensures that in the immediate context children are receiving a good service, but can also encourage parents to have appropriately high expectations of public and private child-care provision.

Working with child(ren) and parents together

The aims of most family centres mean that much of their work is undertaken with parents and children together. There are a number of stages, explored earlier, through which a centre's contact with a family will move from assessment to termination. A child perspective should be included at every stage of the process. This should be demonstrated not only in the aims of the work but also in the detail of the processes. For example, a family with a 3-year-old may be referred for play sessions because of concern over absence of stimulation. In establishing a contract with the family with an agreed goal of increasing the parents' ability to play with their child, agreement may also be sought about ground rules for sessions, such as not discussing the child(ren) negatively in their presence.

Work with whole families where the children are older may utilise family therapy or incorporate insights from such an approach. Where the children are young then sessions involving child(ren) and parents together are more likely to use the medium of play. In setting up such work, thought needs to be given to the appropriate venue for the sessions. The advantages of work in the family's home include easier transfer of learning, a more natural environment for providing an accurate assessment of the parent–child interaction and a setting in which the family may feel more at ease in 'their territory'. These positives need to be weighed against the difficulties of coping with interruptions such as neighbours calling, or the presence of more distractions for child(ren) and parents over which the worker has less control.

Choices about materials will obviously rest on the aim of the sessions. Hence, an aim of promoting a parent's involvement in play would utilise resources either readily available in the family's home or which the centre could lend to the family. Selection of materials and activity also needs to take into account not only their appropriateness to the child's age but also whether they encourage cooperative rather than competitive interaction.

Appropriate parental involvement in activities with their child(ren) may take some time to promote. Many parents lacked the opportunity to play in their own childhoods and thus have to learn to play themselves. Initially their reaction may be to view it as 'silly' or 'strange' and be too embarrassed or uncomfortable to participate. They may need to experience the earliest stage of 'solitary' play before they can join their child in 'cooperative' play. In the early stages of a parent learning to play the involvement of their 'inner' child may result in their competing with their 'real' child. This may be demonstrated by a determination to win a game or their fierce objection to their son or daughter contributing to the parent's painting and 'spoiling' it.

A worker engaging parent and child may frequently find a tension in seeking to address both parties' needs. Although the aim of the work may be primarily to ensure that the child's needs are being met, it may be necessary to pay some attention to the parent at the beginning of each session. Meeting the parent's need early in a session may then enable him/her to focus on the child and his/her needs.

Example 6.3

Carol, a lone parent, was referred to Fulford by the local authority social worker with the aim of improving her relationship with her two young children. She was very reluctant to attend the centre but agreed to a worker holding play sessions with her and the children at home. In the early sessions Carol would often pay little attention to the children and would seek to engage the worker constantly in discussion of Carol's many problems and concerns. Whilst their mother was demanding the worker's attention with urgent conversation, the children would demonstrate their need of adult attention by a variety of angry or tearful behaviour. The worker established an agreement whereby she gave Carol five minutes at the beginning of each session to recount any urgent issues or feelings whilst the rest of the session focused on the children.

A worker's relationship with a family comprises a number of relationships with individual members. One of the aims will always be promoting a positive relationship between parent(s) and child(ren). This requires sensitive intervention by the workers to ensure that they do not inadvertently undermine the relationship they seek to improve. Unthinkingly, a worker may encourage the child's attachment to them at the expense of the parent–child bond. Often there is a good worker–child relationship so that during sessions, if a parent is preoccupied or neglectful of the child's needs, inevitably the child may turn to the worker seeking satisfaction. Remembering the long-term aim of the work may enable the worker to cope with the stress of witnessing the child's distress while not responding to it themselves but drawing the parent's attention to the need and encouraging their response. The worker's strategy will obviously depend on the stage of the work, the needs of the child and the current capacity of the parent. There may be times when a worker decides s/he should respond to the child both for the child's sake and to provide the parent with a model to follow. But for much of the time the worker's role will be indirectly meeting the child's needs through nurturing the parent and his/her 'inner' child.

Many parents require help in thinking about their child's needs and understanding their child's behaviour. In family sessions a worker is provided with immediate events through which learning can take place through the worker's careful feedback to the parents. S/he may need to interpret the child's behaviour to the parents and encourage them to empathise and see things through 'the child's eyes'. When working with families with older children then encouragement can be given to parents and child(ren) to talk and listen to each other.

Working with groups of children and parents

There may be a range of contexts in which a centre works with groups of parents and children. These may be clustered into two main categories of closed and open groups. Some of the major issues were explored in an earlier chapter so this section will focus mainly on the implications for work with children. In setting ground rules for groups containing parents and children a vital component is responsibility for the children. As a group develops it may be important to encourage group responsibility and support for the children, although this should not be at the expense of the individual parent's responsibility. Parents may need the worker's assistance in thinking about norms which recognise children's needs. For example, it may be important to establish group agreement that children will not be discussed critically whilst they are present. Depending on the composition of the group, and the degree to which the parents demonstrate considerable need, the worker(s) may need to be spokesperson(s) for the children.

Locating adult responsibility for the child can be difficult yet essential where centres provide day care/education sometimes with parents present and sometimes with them absent.

Parents may assume that staff are responsible and wait for them to respond to their child whilst staff are expecting a parental response. This can also be confusing for the child so it is vital that the issue of responsibility is discussed in very practical terms with parents for example, who will change/ toilet the child(ren), comfort them when distressed, share in their play, etc.

Group settings may often be used by centres to assess parenting skills and difficulties. Staff need to recognise the impact of an assessment role, particularly in the early stages of work with a group. It will inevitably provoke anxiety in the parent and may lead to atypical behaviour in both parent and child. A parent who has been complaining about his/her child's behaviour may set out to prove how difficult the child is. Workers need to tune in to parents' assumptions about staff (and other parents') expectations of children's behaviour. Some parents may assume that their children will be required to be quiet or passive and seek to repress their child's usual behaviour.

Example 6.4

In an early session of a group for families focusing on parenting skills 3-year-old Marie had a temper tantrum. Her mother, sensing group disapproval, immediately tried to force Marie to stop screaming and kicking. This intensified Marie's behaviour. The worker asked Marie's mother how she would deal with the situation at home and learnt that she would usually ignore the behaviour. She then encouraged the group to share ways of dealing with temper tantrums. This was followed by individual members identifying how they would like to respond to difficult behaviour from their child during sessions. The worker sought agreement from the group that they would support each other in pursuing the individually identified responses.

Parents may be faced with undertaking some arduous and painful work when focusing on their parenting capacities.

Understandably this may lead to their seeking ways to avoid the work. One avoidance activity may be to focus on their child at a time when the programme requires them to meet in a parents' group without the children. Workers may observe that a parent is making it difficult for his/her child to settle in the children's group. This obviously presents problems for the child when the parent is giving very mixed messages of 'I want you to stay in this room without me but it will be very upsetting for both of us'.

Decisions about activities for parent/child groups will be influenced by factors similar to those explored in the previous section. The programme for sessions with a number of parents and children needs to incorporate activities which will engage both children and adults. Again, as indicated earlier, the promotion of cooperation as opposed to competition may be a factor to consider. Similarly attention may need to be paid to appropriate ways to handle parents' desires to create things and their intolerance of their child(ren)'s involvement which in their view mars the creation.

Paramountcy of the child's welfare

The majority of family centres will have the paramountcy of the child's welfare as an underlying value to their work. When much work in a family centre involves working with both parents and children it is not always a simple matter to pursue this fundamental aim. Centres need to think about how to encourage a corporate acceptance of this aim by all staff and parents who, with the children, comprise the family centre. This can be achieved by frequent discussions and debates about the needs and rights of children and how these can be met. Allocating responsibility for oversight of the centre's work with children to individual members of staff can also ensure that a child perspective is always preserved within a staff team.

7

Partnership with Parents

Background to partnership

The concept of partnership with parents has developed over several years and some of the influencing factors are also features which led to the evolution of family centres as outlined in Chapter 2. Thus parental involvement in education has been urged by official reports from Plowden (1967) to Taylor (1977). The 1978 Warnock Report, which was concerned with children with special needs, actually used the word partnership to describe the appropriate relationship between parents and professionals. In the social welfare field, the Seebohm Report (1968) and the Barclay Report (1982) urged consideration of ways of involving clients in decision-making and service-delivery.

There is more than one philosophy underlying partnership with parents. It is sometimes not clear whether partnership is being advocated in the interest of parents, professionals, both, or even neither. Participation is encouraged by a consumer rights movement and by concerns that public services should be accountable to the community. Daines *et al.* (1990) point out that citizen participation may have extensive roots but recent decades have seen a resurgence of interest. They state:

> the general arguments are for citizen involvement but in the welfare field this has been transformed into a new role for service users and especially a role for parents, when the services are for children (Daines *et al.*, 1990, p. 44).

The principle of partnership is now implicit in legislation as the Children Act 1989 Guidance and Regulations (volume 2) indicates when outlining the Act's purview:

> All these provisions reflect the Act's philosophy that the best place for the child to be brought up is usually in his own family and that the child in need (who includes the child with disabilities) can be helped most effectively if the local authority, working in partnership with the parents, provides a range and level of services appropriate to the child's needs.

There are two main and distinct aspects to partnership with parents as Daines *et al.* (1990) suggest. Partnership can occur first at a personal and second at an organisational level and this chapter will examine both aspects.

Partnership with the individual/family

The extract from the Children Act Guidance and Regulations suggests that the reason for partnership is to ensure a more effective meeting of a child's need. From this perspective partnership is a means rather than an end in itself. This is similarly suggested by the definition of partnership provided by Mittler (1983):

> Partnership involves a sharing of knowledge, skills and experience. A commitment to partnership rests on the assumption that children will learn and develop better if parents and professionals are working together on a basis of equality than if either is working in isolation.

That this has not always been the ethos of the relationship between professionals and parents is reflected in the Court Committee's report (Committee on Child Health Services, 1976):

> The growth in the number and variety of professions connected with child-rearing, however necessary in our kind of society, has in some measure undermined the self-confidence of parents . . .

Pugh and De'Ath (1984) write of 'the crushing effect that professional "expertise" has often had, albeit unwittingly, on many parents' views of their own capabilities'.

The DHSS (1985) sponsored research, relating to decisions in child care, reveals both the absence and presence of partnership qualities in social worker–client relationships:

> Concern about the gulf between the values and expectations of social workers and their clients and about problems of communication between them runs throughout the reports.

This contrasted with the characteristics which parents valued in social workers:

> What was appreciated most was honesty, naturalness, and reliability along with an ability to listen. Clients appreciated being kept informed, having their feelings understood, having the stress of parenthood accepted and getting practical help as well as moral support. The social worker whose assistance was valued had a capacity to help parents retain their role as responsible, authority figures in relation to their children.

Literature suggests that most family centres are committed to a philosophy of partnership with their users. Elements of partnership include respect, valuing the individual, openness and honesty. Such attitudes are demonstrated through active involvement of parents (and children where age makes it appropriate) in each stage of the centre's contact with the family. Thus relevant members of the family are engaged in planning, carrying out and evaluating their own programmes and are active and influential participants in written agreements and reviews.

A Fulford Family Centre (1991) parent reported:

> The relationship with the family centre is more of a partnership. The family centre listen to what you are saying. I know that I can see the records kept on me – this reflects their openness. I get a straight answer from family centre workers and I trust them totally.

Research by Daines *et al.* (1990) suggests that friendliness between parents and users is a prerequisite for participation. They explore some confusions that occur between friendliness and friendship and argue that:

> Friendliness, however, involves some reciprocity and will mean that workers need to feel free to share something of themselves with users, parents and colleagues in other agencies. Failing to share one's own beliefs and the facts of one's life, creates distance between people which is uncomfortable, and will detract from participation. But such sharing must be controlled (Daines *et al.*, 1990).

Partnership can easily be rhetoric rather than reality and the impact of differences in power has to be acknowledged. There are more obstacles to establishing a partnership with a parent whose child is the subject of child-protection procedures or a court order or whom the court requires to attend the family centre than there are with the parents who refer themselves to the centre for assistance with difficulties which they have identified.

Organisational partnership

An exploration of organisational partnership with parents will begin with some illustrations from Fulford family centre:

Example 7.1

(a) Fulford Family Centre was set up by Barnardo's, an organisation which in policy statements espouses partnership both as a fundamental value and method. Staff employed to establish the centre were given considerable leeway in interpreting what partnership would mean in practice. They began by canvassing a number of parents in the proposed area, as to the unmet needs of young families which a centre might address and the services they would like to see provided by a family centre. The views elicited were given high priority in planning the

centre programme although they were not the sole deter-
minants of the eventual activities offered.

In the early stages, a considerable amount of workers'
time was spent establishing and supporting a drop-in for
local families. At each drop-in session, time was set aside
for a more formal meeting between workers and parents
when the purpose was to share information, discuss
changes in the drop-in which either parents or workers
felt needed to be made and to talk about other needs and
potential services. Over a period, an identifiable group of
parents, almost entirely women, began to emerge who
were responding to the offer of participation in deciding
which services the centre should offer. They were responding with whole-hearted interest, making criticisms
and concrete suggestions. New groups began to run as a
result of their ideas. One self-help group was set up jointly
by a parent and a worker.

There were two problems with this method of participation. First, users of centre services other than drop-in
tended not to be part of this group, which workers therefore viewed as unrepresentative. In addition, members of
this group were only aware of those parts of the centre's
life in which they themselves were involved. In the
workers' view this meant that they gave undue priority to
those parts of the programme in any discussion about
services.

So the workers therefore devised three alternative
models of a more formal structure for user-involvement.
These models were put to users at two open public meetings and by a majority vote the following structure was
agreed:

● Each of the main aspects of the centre's activities
would be overseen by a committee of users and a
worker.
● A parents' council made up of representatives from the
committees would meet both separately and together
with the staff team at regular intervals to formulate
policy.

(b) After the parents' council had been meeting for more

than a year workers and parents agreed to review how it was going. Workers felt that there ought to be a fixed limit on how long a person should be on the parents' council. They were concerned that recent activities were not represented on the council and they thought more parents should have the opportunity to serve on the council. In addition they believed that some very articulate parents made it difficult for others to get involved and they heard this opinion voiced by some users. Most members of the parents' council saw things differently. They felt that they had only just begun to work together and were just beginning to gain strength through their collaboration. They pointed out that the staff group had a permanent identity and constitution and that they thought this gave the workers a lot of power compared with them. They felt extremely threatened by the workers' proposal and consequently voted them down.

(c) When the Social Fund was introduced, the centre in consultation with users, decided to employ 'aggressive advocacy' in its relations with the DSS. In the opinion of the workers, this should include not only a refusal to assist with applications for loans rather than grants, but also a refusal to turn to charities for needs which had hitherto been met by DSS payments. However, although the consulted users fully approved the policy of advising only on claiming community care grants as opposed to loans, they felt that needs were far too pressing ever to countenance the restricted use of charities. So a policy of assistance only in claiming community care grants and of charitable applications entirely at users' discretion was adopted.

These 'stories' have been recounted, not because they represent practice in all family centres, nor because they are 'typical' of a particular model of centre, but rather because they illustrate issues which will inevitably arise whenever family centres try to put into practice the principle of partnership with parents on more than a personal level. The very fact that the nature of much family centre work means that

workers as a group enter a relationship with groups of families, raises the question of how the inevitable issues of power
and shared purpose within a group are to be handled.

In literature on family centres the involvement of users has
been a constant theme. Holman (1988, p. 185) writes:

> nearly all the centres put a great emphasis on encouraging users
> to regard themselves as participants rather than merely recipients
> . . . The participation of people who had previously regarded
> themselves as failures did much to boost their feelings of self-
> worth, and in so doing enabled them to cope better as parents and
> citizens.

Phelan (1983) states, 'the concept of giving users the chance to
shape policy is part of family-centre philosophy'.

Accounts of emphasis on user-participation in centres tend
to relate to voluntary-sector centres whereas many centres are
run by a local authority. Because of the scarcity of literature
on local authority centres it is not apparent whether organisational partnership is a priority theme for such centres. It is
clear that the flavour of the extracts quoted arises from a
combination of bold assertions and strong aspirations, and is
thus deeply ideological. As Phelan (1983) notes, 'many centre
staff . . . came to their jobs with notions of client power which
they actually incorporated into their objectives'.

Against partnership

It would be rare to find literature on family centres arguing
against partnership but examination of three opposing arguments brings out specific implications. The first views partnership as cooption and defines relations between any welfare
service agency and its users as fundamentally an aspect of
relations between the (bourgeois) state and the working class.
It propounds that in the interests of the working class these
relations need to be as openly antagonistic on the surface of
things as they are in reality. As Hallett (1987) quoting from
Coit (1978) explains:

> 'participationism' tends to eliminate the notion of antagonism

between the working and ruling classes. Participation emphasises the cooperation of these groups with the administration.

Therefore, when agencies offer partnership to their users, they are in effect offering a false view of the nature of class relations. In doing so, they are acting against the interests of their users by encouraging compromise and enlisting active local people to the aims of the agency rather than putting the resources of the agency at the disposal of local people.

A second argument is that it is illegitimate. Insofar as it means family centre workers becoming more accountable to their users, it is perverting the processes of democracy. Rather than being accountable to the groups using the centre at any particular time, workers are in fact accountable to their agencies who are in turn accountable for how they spend public money. In the context of local and central government this means accountability ultimately to local and national electorates. Thus any increase in participation by users in the policy-making of the agency is therefore a diminution of the democratic control of the majority.

The third argument is that it is unwarranted. We do not want partnership when we receive a service from a lawyer or a plumber, so why when we receive a service from a family centre? What people want is the best possible service, not to be involved in running it! It may be important to establish ways of users providing feedback on services but that is a long way away from users making decisions about policy or being asked to organise activities. Associated with this argument would be the assertion that involving users in the provision of services is exploitation of their free labour.

Like most specious arguments, these are useful in that each contains truths that should warn us to beware of enthusiasms for partnership that change nothing. Responding to each argument in turn, there seems no evidence that cooption is being pursued as a malign strategy. It is perfectly true that a stable, relatively organised group which controls the resources is always likely to set the agenda for a relatively unorganised group of shifting membership but there are ways in which this can be addressed.

It is evident that it would be quite illegitimate for centre workers to be wholly accountable to a specific group of users at any particular time. But the argument that accountability runs smoothly from agencies to the state to the electorate is so patently ideological that it has to be regarded as dubious. For most people this theory of democracy is far removed from their experienced reality where governments are rarely representative of the majority. Trying to involve actual and potential users in the complex of interests to which workers are accountable is a way of making accountability more real.

It is likely that most users of family centres do not enter looking for partnerships or intending to become volunteers and that the centre will have many purposes that are not theirs. It is also true that not all participants in centres will desire or have the energy to want to be involved in organisational partnership. But it is also true that the resemblance between users of a family centre and clients of plumbers or lawyers (except in the case of some law centres) is illusory. Because of social structural issues, the relationship of family centre users to the centre and to each other raises questions of power: the relation of children to parents, men to women, white people to black people, working-class people to the state and its agencies – all of these are at the heart of the difficulties which family centres exist to tackle. While it may be true that most of us want the best possible service without any involvement in directing it, it is an open question whether without doing so we will ever get it.

Whilst these arguments can be dismissed, to varying degrees, they are useful in pointing out some of the possible pitfalls in the application of the idea of partnership. In the illustrations given earlier, cooption (who decided representativeness), disputed accountability (who should have had the final say in the debate over charities) and unwarranted expectations of partnership could all be found.

Why partnership?

Having examined some arguments against partnership it is necessary to seek some clarification as to why organisational partnership is valued and pursued. A number of reasons can be offered:

- Consumers of services have a right to shape those services.
- Families have essential knowledge of their own and neighbours' needs and resources.
- Users are empowered by experiences of influence and control which better equip them to participate in other arenas where decisions are made with extensive impact on their lives.
- The services offered by a centre are more likely to be appropriate, responsive and effective if users participate in their planning, provision and evaluation.

Defying definition

It may seem a rather late stage in this chapter to be seeking definitions of partnership. However, the prior examination of some of the issues surrounding it may prove helpful in searching for clear meanings, for as Daines *et al.* (1990) point out, 'partnership benefits, as does participation, from its ambiguity'. The National Children's Bureau have examined and promoted partnership with parents in preschool services, and reporting on their study, Pugh and De'Ath (1989) comment 'Partnership, both in theory and in practice, is a complex and elusive concept.' A definition arising from this research is:

> *Partnership* – a working relationship that is characterised by a shared sense of purpose, mutual respect and the willingness to negotiate. This implies a sharing of information, responsibility, skills, decision-making and accountability (Pugh and De'Ath, 1989).

Daines *et al.* (1990), after examination of different definitions of partnership, suggest that it contains three elements of mutual support, alliance and control. Partnership is viewed by some writers as one of several forms of relationship between professionals and users. Thus Pugh and De'Ath (1989) sees partnership as one of several categories of parental involvement:

> Non-participation – this may be an active decision not to partici-

	pate or it may be passive where a parent may like to participate but be unable to.
External support –	parents may support the centre from outside by fund raising or providing materials.
Participation –	parents may contribute to the centre as helpers or learners.
Partnership –	which is further subdivided into; partnership between individual parent and professional, partnership between parents in general and a particular scheme, partnership between individual parents as workers, and a particular centre; partnership between parents and policy-makers in the community.
Control.	

In some frameworks partnership is placed in a hierarchy of relationships relating to the degree of power held by both parties. From a wider consideration of citizen participation, Arnstein (1972) places partnership as a stage towards citizen control:

8 Citizen control
7 Delegated power
6 Partnership
5 Placation
4 Consultation
3 Informing
2 Therapy
1 Manipulation.

Arnstein's ladder of participation focuses on power and what needs to be clear in any discussion of partnership is that power is a central element. Brown and Clough (1989) refer to partnership as 'another vogue term referring to a relationship between users and staff which offers varying degrees of real power and control to users'. For many workers one of the strongest reasons for pursuing partnership arises from their belief in empowerment. One of the evident ways in which organisational partnership can involve empowerment is through workers and organisation actively giving and sharing power with users.

Factors which promote or prevent partnership

Studies by Pugh *et al.* (1987) and by Daines *et al.* (1990) demonstrate the frequency of a gulf between aims and achievements in partnership. Liffman (1978) provides a fascinating account of a family centre project in Australia which had at the outset an aim of handing over control to its users. His account demonstrates both the triumphs and the difficulties in achieving this aim:

> Open settings, equal relationships, authentic human encounters, willingness to meet actual client demand: these modes of practice were under constant threat of subversion by traditional or innovative behavioural and organisational barriers.

So what encourages and what impedes partnership? There are a number of relevant factors: organisational context, model of centre, worker attitudes and skills, strategies and structures.

Organisational context

Issues such as sources of funding, accountability for the centre within a wider organisation, management structure and style are all influential elements. There may be more freedom for family-centre staff to embark on organisational partnership in a centre sponsored by a voluntary body than in one under the auspices of the local authority. Funding agencies may place requirements on a centre in terms of partnership with users. A democratic style of user involvement in decision-making may be difficult for staff to maintain if they are employed by an organisation which operates an autocratic style of management.

Workers will have a crucial role to play in seeking to influence the wider organisation's commitment to partnership. This dimension cannot be neglected unless workers and users are to face frustration and disillusionment. Parents will become disheartened and dissuaded from participation if they belatedly discover that the wider organisation is seeking, not their decisions, but their opinions – which are subsequently discarded.

Model of centre

As demonstrated earlier, there are many and varied models of family centre and partnership is more feasible with some models than with others. Centres whose aims, objectives and programme are tightly prescribed will have limited areas in which they can offer genuine organisational partnership. A wide geographical area and lack of ready access to the centre for families are also obvious factors which inhibit partnership. In contrast, a neighbourhood-based centre with open access will find it easier to facilitate partnership with users.

Worker attitudes and skills

Just as the organisation must be clear about the extent of partnership, so too the workers need to be clear about the degree of power and control they possess and the extent to which they are willing to share it with users. Attitudes towards parents outlined in the section on personal partnership are essential to the promotion of partnership. Approaches which cling to the need to be an 'expert'; which seek to do things to people rather than with or alongside them; which value professional knowledge and skill more highly than personal wisdom and local experience are examples of attitudes which are the antithesis of partnership.

Some staff may find partnership difficult and two of the sources of difficulty may be lack of confidence and feelings of powerlessness. A lack of confidence leads a staff member to hold on to the 'expert' role. There can be a destructive and unconscious bolstering of self-esteem which is obtained by undermining and undervaluing a parent's contribution in contrast to the professional's skill. Workers encouraged, or in some settings required, to work in partnership are likely to be the least powerful within an organisation and may be reluctant to share the limited power they hold.

The espousal of partnership in the family centre movement, without help and support for staff to pursue it, can be stressful and counter-productive. Thus Tristam (1986) recounts how at a meeting of the Association of Scottish Family Centres, 'it was apparent that feelings of guilt and inadequacy could easily be induced in those workers whose Units were low on evidence of partnership and control'. Hence the promotion of partnership requires training and support for staff, which encompasses attitudes, values, knowledge and skills. The primary skills in partnership may be those of enabling and empowering.

Any centre aiming at partnership needs to take stock of its progress. Staff committed to partnership still need to examine their ways of working regularly. There can be habitual, perhaps invisible/unconscious ways in which staff erect blocks to partnership. These may be untested assumptions about 'the way things work' or messages received by parents about the busyness and unavailability of staff. The study already referred to by Liffman (1978) explores how in a centre, deeply committed to an aim of user-control and thus of a radical transformation of the relationship between staff and user, there was still a strong tendency for the characteristics of the conventional professional/client relationship to reassert themselves.

Strategies and structures

Genuine attempts at partnership with parents need to be grounded in strategies and participatory structures. As Liffman (1978) reports from his study of the Family Centre Project in Melbourne:

> for participation to be more than a lofty ideal it was necessary that specific structures and mechanisms be created, the more so because families were unused to the idea of participation and knew little about formalised decision-making processes.

Parents' unfamiliarity with partnership and lack of experience requires the provision of opportunities for parents to gain knowledge and skills. Appropriate training courses may be provided by adult education agencies which introduce users to the skills involved in participating in and managing meetings.

Creation of participatory structures requires careful thought and planning. How will they be established and how will representative membership be obtained? Clearly if much of a centre's work entails groups of families, the groups form ready-made constituencies on which representation can be based. A centre where the majority of work with families is carried out on an individual basis has a much harder task of first establishing a parental forum with which organisational partnership can be pursued. Users are rarely a homogeneous group so how will fair representation be achieved which takes cognisance of race and gender?

The procedure for obtaining representation also needs consideration. Parents may express interest in serving on a parents' committee or council but lack the confidence to stand in an election. Elections are by nature competitive and can be divisive. In the early stages of encouraging participatory structures, parents may prefer a system which gives everyone an equal chance of selection such as drawing names from a hat.

Management of meetings requires that there are explicit procedures. Are decisions to be reached on the basis of consensus or through a voting system? Liffman (1978) is illuminating when he recounts the effect of a staff group's unclear way of reaching decisions on the families' subsequent attempts to resolve issues:

> One of the most difficult challenges for the families, as they moved into new decision-making roles, was to learn how to 'agree to disagree'. The staff's subtle approaches to this were too intangible to be readily learned by families. More structured and visible ways of dealing with disagreements within the staff body might have assisted the families to cope later with disagreements within the committee and thus obviate the chaos, brawls and resignations that so troubled it in its earliest days.

Disagreements between parents, between parents and staff, and between members of staff are inevitable and the handling of conflict is a critical issue in the pursuit of partnership. If controversy is to be creative rather than destructive it must be acknowledged and a collaborative problem-solving stance needs to be taken as opposed to a win/lose approach.

The titles chosen for publications on partnership by Daines *et al.* (1990), *Aiming for Partnership*, and by Pugh and De'Ath (1989), *Working towards Partnership in the Early Years*, both indicate the difficulties in achieving partnership. The complexities in managing the divide between the ideal and the real is apparent in the final page of Daines *et al.* (1990), who state:

> We agree with Mittler (1983) that partnership with parents is an essential but unachievable aim but would not want, by making clear that partnership is (under present structures) unachievable, to undermine the commitment of staff who are working towards it. We believe strongly that social welfare projects should be aiming towards partnership.

They conclude that the word 'partnership' should be dropped and that: 'maximum feasible participation' should prove a testing enough goal.

On the one hand this may be seen as a realistic resolution of the inherent difficulties, but on the other hand it may provide too ready an excuse for organisations and staff to avoid the arduous demands of transforming the relationships of professionals and agencies to their participants/users, through tackling issues of power and control. Whether an unattainable goal, a style of working or an essential approach, partnership remains a challenging concept for all family centres to pursue.

8

Management Issues (I)

What is management?

Pick up any two books on management and you will read two different definitions of management. Heller (1972) accounts for the variety by suggesting, 'any definition of management must be right, because almost any definition must fit something so amorphous and shifting'. There appears to be greater agreement about the functions of management; most writers suggesting that they include planning, organising, leading and controlling. Drucker (1977, p. 28) ascribes three tasks to management:

1. to fulfil the specific purpose and mission of the organisation;
2. to make work productive and the worker achieving;
3. to manage social impacts and responsibilities.

The language of management can sometimes seem to be alien and uncomfortable to those involved in a social service. As Handy (1988) points out, the origins of much of the language is found in engineering but he suggests:

> Things are changing, however. The new words in the organizational literature are words like, 'culture', 'shared values', 'networks and alliances', 'power and influence', 'federalism', 'compromise and consent' and most crucially, 'leadership' rather than 'management' (Handy, 1988, p. 21).

But organisations responsible for the provision of family

133

centres may find they cannot ignore the other more unfamiliar language as public and voluntary bodies become increasingly required to define 'targets' and 'inputs' and measure 'outcomes' and 'outputs'.

Many models of management are available, with varying degrees of relevance to the immediate centre manager and those involved in its management 'at a distance', such as management committee members or managers at middle or senior level in the sponsoring organisation. Stewart (1992) counsels the public sector not to develop models of management based on the private sector. Regardless of their origins, what a lot of models describe is a fairly static approach where everything fits and follows with some logic. Thus they suggest: be clear about your purpose and mission; from this define your operational objectives; ensure staff resources are adequate and equipped to meet these; provide and control physical and financial resources again to meet the objectives; measure outcomes; ensure quality; recheck your purpose and mission; refine your objectives and so on and so forth.

Often what seems to be missing in this neat approach is the reality of life in the family centre: the problems and crises of the human situations people face; the reality of under-funding, short-term funding and cutbacks; the real cost and stress on staff; and the new legislation or local policy decisions. All will change the centre's carefully worked-out mission 'at a stroke'. A vital ingredient of family centre management is the approach to crisis, flux and the management of change. Family centres are far from alone in this, but because of their small size organisationally and their close contact with the service participants, the effects of crisis and change can be the more dramatic and at times terminal.

However, without the frameworks established of mission and objectives, and of evaluation through outcomes and quality measurement, the vagaries of crisis and change are far less likely to be weathered or survived and successful management of the change will not occur. A basic approach to these necessary frameworks is outlined below but first a brief consideration of some of the broader issues which relate to managing a family centre.

Organisational contexts and constraints

As indicated earlier, family centres are sponsored and managed by a variety of agencies. This results in diverse organisational contexts and constraints. As can be imagined, there are likely to be considerable differences between a small self-help centre with a management committee, a family centre jointly financed and managed with a view to transferring resources to control by local-users and a family centre managed by a large local authority. A majority of family centres are small units belonging to large organisations. Each centre will be influenced by particular aspects of the wider organisational structure, such as the degree of decentralisation and the extent of a hierarchy. Organisations have both different structures and cultures which will affect the amount of freedom and autonomy of a centre.

Power and control

Whether conscious or not, the organisation and its managers who set up and operate a family centre exercise immense power; power that is unlikely to be relinquished or shared to more than just a limited degree with other stakeholders – or to any degree at all unless there is a conscious and explicit aim to do so.

The power inherent in setting and defining the objectives of the centre and the control exercised over developments and operation through resource allocation (staff, money and buildings) is considerable in its effect on families. It can be used to ensure a particular interpretation of people's lives and problems, it can be used to maintain people's experience of disadvantage or role in society. It can individualise inequality and be blind to its own maintenance of the structural causes of inequality. For example, a lack of race-awareness, and of explicit strategies to combat racism, can lead a centre to be welcoming and appropriate only for white families and white staff, excluding black families and black staff from access to and influence over its resources. Too often the focus in centres can confirm women's traditional roles and disadvantages, but also exclude men from the opportunity for change in their own perception of self, role and attitudes. For all, unless there are overt approaches that aspire to empowerment and partnership, the centre will confirm users as being only recipients of services on the goodwill or patronage of the organisation, management and staff of the centre.

A statement of values and principles that underpin a centre's operation is not in itself sufficient to direct the power positively or even begin to share it. It is however an essential first step in acknowledging its existence. Specific strategies need to be developed and included in aims, objectives and targets to ensure those values and principles are put into practice. Monitoring and evaluation processes are necessary to ensure that standards are met.

Issues that need consideration in producing a statement of values and principles in a family centre would include:

- the rights of the child;
- the rights and responsibilities of parents;
- Anti-discriminatory principles on:
    race
    gender
    disability
    sexuality;
- Partnership.

The work done on values and principles through strategic thinking and planning will help not only to define the culture and climate of the centre, but also, in itself, to achieve specific objectives.

Aims and objectives

In setting objectives a fundamental question, which relates to power and control, asks who is involved in the process? The range of those who might participate is considerable, spanning managers in the wider organisation or members of a management committee; the centre manager; the other centre staff; the families using the centre; the funders who may be separate from the organisation managing the centre; and other interested agencies. A principle of partnership and the need to ensure commitment to objectives requires that participant families and staff are included.

Even before detailed aims and objectives are set a survey of need can be undertaken in the local area where new or changed provision for a family centre is planned. The population for the survey will depend on the outline plans. Under the Children Act 1989 local authorities are required to identify the extent to which there are 'children in need' in their area. A local authority's findings may be an important contribution to a family centre's survey. If a centre is to target families in particular difficulty, it might be possible to ask members of families currently or previously involved with the local social services office what services they think would help families. If a centre is to be neighbourhood-based with open access, then it is necessary to seek the views of a cross-section of local parents so that realistic and helpful services can be provided. It is only through such a process that the dangers of a group of professionals providing unwanted services can be avoided.

A consumer study can clarify what potential centre users will find relevant and useful and thus inform the aims and objectives. As stated earlier, clear aims and objectives will not eliminate the effects of crisis and sudden change, but they are essential as the basis through which change can be managed and a reasonable focus maintained, in an environment where it is too easy to be all things to all people and achieve nothing.

The work undertaken by the National Institute for Social Work in setting aims and developing specific objective trees is invaluable as a framework (see, for example, Douglas and Payne, 1988; Miller and Scott, 1984). They suggest an approach to setting objectives which defines specific goals in concrete, measurable terms. It divides into three areas, impacts, services and logistics (see Figure 8.1).

Objectives in each of the three areas are defined at three different levels:

Banner   this level gives an overall 'mission' type statement.

Theme   this groups objectives according to specific areas of activity or approach

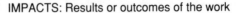

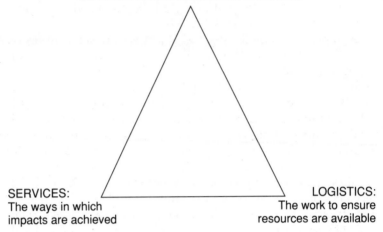

Figure 8.1 *The 'objectives triangle'* (Douglas and Payne, 1988) © National Institute for Social Work, reproduced with permission.

Operational this describes detailed and precise activity targets in very concrete and measurable terms.

The process provides a 'tree' of objective statements which offer a clear framework for the operational management of the centre, and shared purpose and goals for staff and participants (see Figure 8.2).

The aims and objectives need to identify the target population for whom services and activities are to be designed. This requires answers to such detailed questions as:

(a) What is the geographical/catchment area?
(b) What is the age structure of families that the centre is designed to deal with?
(c) Is the centre for all families in the area who fit the criterion of age structure or is it primarily for those facing greatest 'stress'?
(d) If the centre is for families with particular difficulties or under greatest 'stress', how are the difficulties or stress defined? For instance, definitions could include families with children defined as 'in need' under the Children Act;

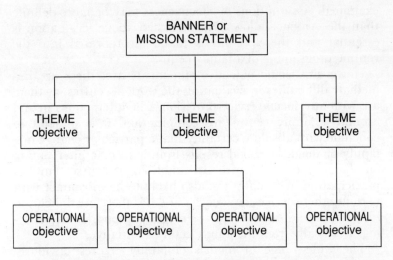

Figure 8.2 *Objectives tree* (Douglas and Payne, 1988) © National Institute for Social Work, reproduced with permission.

having children on the child-protection register; lone parenthood; isolation of the family; inadequate housing; or being totally dependent on state benefit.

Undertaken thoroughly enough and with sufficiently specific statements, the objectives at operational level should provide the basis for monitoring systems, and be capable of delineating standards and quality levels to be achieved. The ability to demonstrate achievement of objectives, to measure outcomes and to assure the standards of the service are essential not only for the scrutiny and involvement of centre participants and other interested parties but also increasingly to ensure survival at the hands of funders.

Evaluation

Although there is optimism about the effectiveness of family centres, the evaluation of centres is still in its infancy. Indeed, the enthusiasm of staff working in family centres might carry with it the danger that methods and effectiveness are not examined. Assumptions of effectiveness may be more definite than the evidence allows. As suggested above, evaluation is essential and therefore needs to be incorporated into the routine programme of a family centre.

However specific objective statements are, there are immediate difficulties in evaluating the work of centres, as there are with any social service provision. The interactions in and around a family centre are complex and it is difficult to conclude with absolute certainty that a particular change in a family or neighbourhood results from a specific intervention on the part of the centre. In addition, of course, families participating in a centre are also likely to be in contact with various other services or agencies and it is therefore difficult to identify alterations in family or neighbourhood life as resulting specifically from the family centre's initiatives.

The wide range of models of family centres obviously necessitates a range of evaluation techniques. Specific changes in family functioning cannot be assessed by a general neighbourhood-based type of evaluation, nor can changes in the environment of bringing up children be assessed through detailed study of the functioning of a small number of families. However, it is possible to produce general guidelines for the evaluation of family centres. In family centre work, as in other social service provision, it is easy for a myth to emerge that evaluation is a particularly complex, demanding and highly skilled activity which only a few can perform. It needs clear guidelines and thinking but it can be and ought to be one of the basic tools and activities of family centre work. It is crucial to stress that the skills necessary to accomplish evaluation are in all likelihood already possessed by family centre staff.

The style of evaluation developed should mirror the ethos of partnership and allow parents to participate fully in it. It should thus incorporate the parents in the centre, not only as subjects of the evaluation but also as partners in exploring the impact of the centre on the families and their neighbourhood.

Quantitative methods

In order to evaluate the efficiency and effectiveness of a family centre, both quantitative indicators and qualitative measurements are needed. The former tend to provide information as to the extent to which a centre is fulfilling its service objectives and the latter relate more to impact objectives. Quantitative indicators would include:

- the level of provision – what and how much;
- the number of families per week, per year, etc.;
- the number and type of contacts with families;
- user-profiles, including indicators such as age, gender, household structure, ethnic origin, etc.

These categories require the establishment of simple systems for recording and collating data. Increasingly, centres may have access to computerised systems which allow the recording of day-to-day practice data to be easily transformed into evaluative information. The maintenance of regular data enables changes in the use of services or in the profile of users to be readily identified.

User-profiles are essential to ensure the target population specified in the aims and objectives is being reached. Where a centre is neighbourhood-based it may be desirable to discover how representative the centre-users are of local families. This first requires an assessment of the characteristics of families living locally. Some demographic information should be available from local census information or area profiles which have been undertaken. These could provide such details as: the number of lone-parent households; the number of households where there is no wage-earner; or the proportion of households with a high number of young children. Equally there may be data about membership of Afro-Caribbean, Asian or other minority ethnic families.

If such information is not available in sufficient detail then it may be necessary to devise a small-scale survey to identify the key characteristics of local families. With adequate time and support, staff in the family centre will be able to do this. It may be appropriate to involve parents already using the family centre in this exercise. Unless a centre has a very small catchment area it will not be realistic to get information on all families and thus efforts must be made to ensure a representative sample is selected. This will need to take into account different types and sizes of accommodation.

Once representative information about the characteristics of the local community is obtained this can be compared with the user-profiles. This comparison may well show that groups in the wider community are not proportionately represented in the centre. For instance, lone parents or families from particular minority ethnic groups may not be using the centre.

This exercise can be extended in terms of the families to whom a centre gives particular priority. Local social services' teams will be able to provide overall information about the number of children in the catchment area on the child-protection register. If these numbers appear comparatively high but are not reflected in the centre's statistics then questions can be asked in terms of the centre targeting those families with children at greatest risk.

If information about user-profiles is combined with the nature and number of contacts this can indicate whether a disproportionate amount of the centre's resources are being spent on particular categories of families. This information makes it possible to assess whether the centre is fulfilling its priorities.

Qualitative evaluation

In addition to quantitative indicators a centre needs to evaluate how far it is meeting its impact objectives and this requires qualitative measurements. Impact objectives spell out the desired effect and change which the centre aims to achieve. This may be impact on individual children or families, or effect on the environment or neighbourhood. Evaluation of a centre's impact on individual families was covered in Chapter 4. Collation of individual evaluations enables a centre to obtain an indication of its effectiveness in achieving its objectives. In addition to routine evaluation of work with individual families, centres may undertake periodic consumer studies to evaluate not only the changes which participants identify within their families as a result of the centre's services, but also their experience of the centre in terms of its values and culture – for instance, the degree of partnership or their perception of its anti-discriminatory practice.

Evaluation of environmental or neighbourhood impact is much harder to measure. As Henderson and Thomas (1989) point out:

> In the United States evaluation in community work, social work and social action programmes have been extensively written about. In Britain little evaluation research has been done in community work or related fields.

Centres whose objectives include neighbourhood effects need to be clear about what they hope to achieve and how the achievements can be measured.

Evaluation also has a key role to play in local debates about how best to use limited resources for the benefit of families. In terms of securing resources the untested crusading zeal of family centre workers is not likely to be as effective as a clear statement of number of families worked with, the characteristics of those families and the direction and extent of change. Rather than something 'added on' to family centre work or completed by outside teams of 'experts', the evaluation of a family centre should be a core responsibility of workers and managers and should involve thoroughly the centre's participants.

9

Management Issues (II)

Staffing

The composition of the staff group

As in most social services establishments, staff are the major resource both as the primary means of service provision and in terms of revenue expenditure. The degree to which careful planning and choice can be exercised in setting up a staff team is obviously constrained by whether or not a family centre is a new venture or the conversion of existing provision. In a new venture recruitment of staff can be tailored to the needs of the enterprise.

The material covered so far in this book will indicate the considerable range of methods and activities which are found in most centres working with families. Skills will usually be shared amongst a staff team, although there are some fundamental competences which are required by all workers whose primary role involves direct work with the families using a centre. These are skills central to social work and certain other similar occupations. The Barclay Report (1982) outlined three categories:

> skills in human relationships; skills in analysis (assessing people, analysing situations and evaluating the effects of action taken); and skills in effectiveness (carrying out action planned) (p. 151).

If a centre is to be effective across a wide spectrum then a breadth of skills and experience needs to be held within the staff team. Most centres work with individuals, families and groups and to varying degrees with the local community. If a staff team includes a range of skills in different methods this enables a greater flexibility in response to need. In order to work effectively with families, the staff team should encompass skills and experience in working both with children and with adults. Staff also need to be able to work with children and parents together.

Because of the pressures of time and necessary breadth of curriculum, few social-work courses provide students with extensive understanding and practice in direct work with children. Conversely, courses providing a qualification for work with children, such as teaching or nursery nursing, can give their students only a limited familiarity with working with adults. A team which includes both staff with a background in working with children and staff with experience of working with adults is likely to be able to maintain the essential duality of both a child- and parent-perspective. It also enables staff to develop essential skills which they lack, through learning from colleagues.

Race and gender are vital aspects of any staff team. Increasingly, employing organisations are practising equal opportunities in employment and many are addressing the under-representation of minority ethnic groups amongst their personnel in their recruitment policies. Centres serving communities which include a variety of ethnic groups have important choices to make when seeking to recruit staff. One way of ensuring that black staff are recruited in a project aiming to provide a service to black families is the use of race as a 'genuine occupational qualification' under the Race Relations Act 1976 (section 5.2.d, posts). The potential benefits and difficulties of this approach need to be recognised. Whilst ensuring the employment of a member of staff of a particular racial group to provide services to that minority group, a danger of this approach is that the black member of staff may be prevented from working with a wide range of centre-users by being required to concentrate on services to black users. In addition the rest of the team may abdicate their responsibilities for both black users and anti-racist practice. Clearly these dangers must be addressed through the management of the team.

As already indicated, for various reasons, the large majority of adult users of centres are mothers. It is likely that centres which include male members of staff have some advantage over all-female staff groups if they are seeking to work with fathers. Male members of staff also have an important function in providing role-models of men caring for children. In a high majority of social-services provision it is women who fulfil the care and domestic roles and men who hold management positions (Langan, 1992).

Consideration needs to be given to the degree to which a staff team is generic, with individuals practising some specialisms, and the extent to which individuals will fulfil varied roles. Some clarity about staff roles is important both for staff and families but clarity need not equal rigidity. Flexibility is often both necessary for providing an effective, responsive service and rewarding to staff in terms of job satisfaction. Responsibility for overseeing or developing a particular aspect of a centre's programme need not equate with sole responsibility for undertaking the work involved.

Effective recruitment and deployment of staff obviously requires appropriate job descriptions and the identification of person specifications, followed by adequate induction of new staff. Where centres are already established or arise from the conversion of existing provision, changes in the balance of staff skills will mainly rely on staff training and development.

The informal approach of many centres and a style of working alongside people can mean that for new users of a centre it can be difficult to identify staff. Whilst a lack of immediate distinguishing features between staff and families may be a sign of effective partnership between them it can also be a source of uncertainty and confusion for newcomers. This can be addressed by providing leaflets or displaying information which includes photographs and names of staff with some explanation of their roles.

The staff as a team

In most family centres staff need to work together as an effective team. First, this improves the work with families, for although there will often be some system of 'keyworking' with families, a typical pattern is for several staff to be in contact with each family. The programme of most family centres, in common with other day and residential establishments, involves staff and families in working together in myriad patterns of groups and groupings. Second, if the most likely way of achieving the necessary breadth of skills is through their distribution within the staff group; then clearly it is vital that the staff collaborate well. Thus if the staff group is to be effective it needs to pay sufficient time and attention to its internal processes and needs to grow and develop.

A staff group with a breadth of skills and experience provides a rich resource for a centre and its families, but its management is not without difficulties. Staff from different disciplines may hold varied philosophies and values whilst an assumption may be made that staff hold a common outlook. Variety in training and previous roles may result in different approaches.

Differences frequently exist not only between different disciplines but also between staff holding the same qualification. There is considerable heterogeneity within the social-work profession; both in terms of underlying philosophies and methods and models of practice. Such differences can be very constructive and stimulating although they also carry the risk of being divisive. As indicated in the chapter on partnership, it is important that a staff team, like any group, views conflict as carrying a constructive potential and finds ways of handling the inevitable disagreements that arise when working together. All groups struggle with the temptation to deny or avoid conflict, but this leads to frustration and loss of energy within the group.

The staff team can spend some fruitful time together exploring members' differing values and assumptions and recognising the implications for working together. What is essential, if any such examination is to be productive, is that the team has a culture of trust and respect for each staff member's unique contribution. Clearly trust is not created within a group overnight but the team manager carries a major responsibility for encouraging its development.

Team managers need to pay attention to issues of inclusion and exclusion and to times of joining and leaving. The staff group in a family centre will be of varying size and will contain both professional and support staff. Thought needs to be given as to who should attend staff meetings and, if regular meetings do not involve the whole staff group, whether occasional gatherings should be planned which include all staff, regardless of role and hours worked. The employment of new staff requires appropriate preparation of the team and induction of the new member(s) of staff. Most centres will provide placements to various training courses particularly social work and nursery nursing and preparation also needs to be undertaken when students are joining the team. Teams, like any group, need to address the tasks and feelings resulting from members leaving the team.

Styles of leadership

If staff are the most important resource of a family centre then their management is also a vital activity. A useful perspective for managing a team is found in recognising that it is a group and that groupwork theory and practice can offer valuable insights to a manager. Groupwork theory propounds that a group has three interrelated areas of need: task needs; group maintenance needs; and the needs of individual group members. These needs have to be balanced and met to a sufficient degree for a group to be productive and for individuals to be satisfied by their group membership. Individuals vary in their awareness of these needs and their propensity to behave in ways which satisfy these needs. Thus some people are task-oriented and consistently fulfil roles in a group which help it to achieve its task (for example, seeking information, clarifying, summarising) whilst others demonstrate an ability to assist the maintenance of a group (encouraging participation, helping communication, harmonising, for instance).

It is probably a rare individual who can undertake a perfect balance of task and maintenance behaviours, but in most groups the necessary functions are distributed among members. Team managers need to recognise the contribution which each member of staff can make to the team's effectiveness through the particular task or maintenance behaviours which they tend to perform. Recognition that these leadership functions are distributed within a group enables a team leader to facilitate other team members' contributions thus enhancing the team's performance and fulfilment for members. It also avoids the danger of believing that a leadership position means being the sole performer of all leadership behaviour.

Much has been written about leadership and it is a topic that team leaders/managers can fruitfully reflect upon. An alternative framework for understanding leadership style is to identify two predominant styles in managers: autocratic/authoritarian and democratic. The primary distinction between these styles rests with the use of power and control. The autocratic manager exercises power by directing and instructing staff on the basis of decisions s/he reaches. The democratic leader shares power and responsibility with the staff group. Research suggests that while autocratic leadership may be effective in task achievement it provides less satisfaction for group/team members and can lead to resentment and dependence. Research described by Shaw (1976) suggests that it may be somewhat easier to be an autocratic than a democratic leader!

Effective styles of leadership are influenced by the context of leadership. In most key aspects of family centre management, a democratic style of leadership is likely to be effective and appropriate. Managers, whether immediate or 'at a distance' cannot expect staff to work in partnership with users if they themselves operate a style of management contrary to partnership principles. Organisations which emphasise rigid hierarchical structures can make democratic management styles difficult to pursue. Daines *et al.* (1990) commenting on their research findings on attempts at partnership in a voluntary agency point out:

> We did not find in this research the kind of invisible wall which seems to be erected in some social services departments between team leaders and their teams, and all middle and senior managers. For such departments, any moves towards user participation would need to be prefaced by a major change in management style (Daines *et al.*, 1990, p. 141).

The manager's style of leadership will often be most apparent in the conduct and function of team meetings. The most appropriate method of conducting the meeting will obviously relate to its purpose. A basic assumption which needs challenging is that the meeting should always be chaired by the team leader/manager. It can be effective to rotate the chair amongst those team-members who wish to undertake the role. It is clear from the format of some meetings that the manager sees them as an opportunity for providing information and possibly obtaining views of staff but not as a decision-making forum.

Care is needed to avoid the two extremes of 'autocratic' team managers confining all decision-making to themselves or '*laissez-faire*' managers leaving the whole team to make all decisions. The former stance leads to inevitable problems in implementing important decisions. Research shows clearly that a group involved in decision-making is more likely to be committed to the implementation. Involvement of the whole team in every decision is time-wasting and frustrating for everyone. It is essential for a team manager to discriminate between team decisions and those appropriately taken individually. Where a team is involved, clarity is required as to whether the decision will be reached by consensus or a majority verdict. The most appropriate method of decision-making will relate to the importance of the decision, the degree of commitment of the team needed to carry it out and the time available.

Individual and team supervision

A family centre's requirement of variety amongst staff in terms of skills and roles has obvious implications for job descriptions, staff recruitment and staff training and development. Managing a staff group where different job descriptions and terms and conditions of service operate poses particular difficulties. These may be most acute where the centre is a partnership between two authorities. Centre managers may find themselves having to operate within particular organisational requirements which seem ill-fitted to the nature of a family centre. Staff with varying background and training may be undertaking very similar roles with families, and such flexibility will usually be of the greatest benefit for families and thus for the employing body. However, a tradition of differential pay and conditions between different professions resulting in staff undertaking similar if not identical work for different rates of pay and even being required to work different hours may lead to tensions.

Staff supervision is a key activity for centre managers. Parsloe (1981) outlines three major components to supervision:

● checking that agency and team policies are being carried out and that work is of an adequate standard;
● enriching the service to the client;
● assisting in the workers' professional development.

Thus supervision is about meeting the clients' needs, the organisation/agency's needs and the workers' needs. As should already be evident, in family centres, agency and team policy and the service to families are carried out through a complex matrix of formal and informal activities. The contexts for activities encompass:

individual worker and individual user;
two workers and a couple or family;
a group of participants and one or more workers.

There are numerous combinations and permutations of these arrangements and each centre participant and each centre worker will experience a specific matrix. The complexity of a family centre, and other day or residential establishments, poses a challenge for supervision.

Traditionally, supervision has taken an individual focus but Payne and Scott (1982) recommend that the entire staff group should be the primary focus for supervision:

> The implication here is that the supervision needs of individuals should be always related to other team members' needs and resources. Individual and collective needs can then be identified in relation to the particular objectives and priorities of the unit (Payne and Scott, 1982, p. 1).

Certainly the nature of family centre work finds such a focus far more meaningful. It is important not to restrict the term 'supervision' to individual meetings between team leader and worker or to presentations of work with individuals/families to a group of staff. In fact a wide range of activities and settings are the means through which the components of supervision are undertaken and it may be difficult to distinguish supervision from management. In their helpful document on supervision of teams, Payne and Scott (1982) suggest five objectives for supervision. Each one is quoted below and then examples are provided of how centres can achieve the objective.

1. *To ensure that the operations of the operational unit are consistent with the primary functions of the agency*

Many of the activities relating to this objective have been referred to earlier as they include setting the family centre's aims and objectives; defining priorities; allocating work; reviewing the centre's policy and practice; evaluating both work with individual families and the overall work of the centre.

2. *To ensure that workers are clear, individually and collectively, about their roles and responsibilities*

This objective is accomplished through individual and team discussion of roles and responsibilities; reviewing both the workload of individual staff and the centre's workload.

3. *To develop a suitable climate and satisfactory conditions for practice*

Activities fulfilling this objective centre on teamwork and team-building, which means giving suitable priority to team meetings and creating a team ethos of trust and confidence to express and resolve conflicts.

4. *To reduce the stresses that are likely to impair effective service delivery*

The nature of family centre work is both rewarding and

stressful. Being regularly and intensively in contact with children and parents struggling with disadvantage and distress or experiencing violence or despair is very demanding. Strategies and practices to ensure that the inevitable stress does not become disabling include:

individual and team discussion and support;
ensuring that leave is taken and overtime avoided wherever possible;
setting aside extended periods for team discussion and reflection.

5. *To assist professional development in terms of*:
   (a) *developing and improving basic skills*,
   (b) *increasing and developing knowledge required for practice*.

These objectives are achieved through:

induction of new staff;
feedback from colleagues about joint or observed work;
staff appraisal and identification of training needs;
encouragement of staff to use a wide range of resources to develop their knowledge and skills and team training events.

Team leaders need to encourage the development of a range of tools and techniques within the team in order to achieve the objectives of supervision. It is essential that they recognise both what the team can contribute and what outside resources such as external consultants can provide and avoid viewing themselves as the sole resource for supervisory activities. Fitzgerald and Walsh (1990) describe a process of providing consultancy to a family centre.

Working with other agencies

Why?

Various reports over many years have exhorted inter-agency cooperation and collaboration. The findings of every child-abuse enquiry emphasise failures in inter-disciplinary communication. It is clear that working effectively with other agencies is no easy task, but it is one which every family centre needs to pursue for the benefit of their participants. It is this which must primarily motivate inter-agency efforts rather than the needs of organisations or individual workers. Section 27 of the Children Act expects local authorities to develop a corporate policy on services for children and families. Thus cooperation between different departments and agencies is envisaged in the Act.

The lives of children and parents are affected by a multiplicity of professional workers and agencies. A family's housing, finance, health, education, recreation and so forth are heavily influenced by a confusing array of public, voluntary and private agencies and authorities. Family centres exist within this complex provision and their participants will gain from the establishment of positive relationships with other relevant agencies.

In addition family centres may be reliant on other agencies for their funding; either through grants or service agreements. It is therefore important that inter-agency avenues are set up for negotiating, implementing and evaluating the service provision and the funding implications.

Who?

The first task in establishing inter-agency relationships is to identify the detail of the formal network to which the centre belongs. The nature of this network will vary according to the purpose and type of family centre. Whilst, as already indicated, the agencies affecting families are numerous it will not be feasible or necessary for a centre to establish equally close working relationships with each agency. The sponsoring agency for the family centre will determine the siting of the centre within the formal network. Thus a centre operating under the auspices of social services will be in a different position and perceived differently from a centre sponsored by an education or health authority. Likewise a centre managed by a voluntary agency will have a different place in the formal network from its statutory or public-sector counterparts.

Centres which result from a partnership between different agencies have particular issues to address in terms of the nature of the partnership.

Family centres have to work with other agencies at a number of different levels and these need to be identified and responsibility for collaboration clarified. Cox and Parish (1989) suggest three levels at which inter-agency relationships may be identified:

- Policy planning level
- Management level
- Operational level

Neglect of any of these levels can limit the effectiveness of provision for families and in some instances even jeopardise the existence of a centre. Responsibility for cooperation at these various levels may rest with different staff but there may be overlap. All centre staff will be involved and share responsibility for good inter-agency relationships at operational level. The centre manager and those responsible for the centre's management 'at a distance' will need to establish collaboration at a management level. This is likely to involve a number of different management positions in other agencies. The policy planning level will obviously be a key stratum when a centre is first established or altered in any major way. In addition, family centres or their senior managers may use 'findings' or issues from a centre's work to contribute to other agencies' policies or service planning for children and families.

How and when?

A number of different processes and procedures need to be established by a family centre for good inter-agency working. These include:

- Channels for consultation about aims, services and activities.
- Processes for circulating accurate information about aims, services and activities to other agencies.

- Methods for circulating within the centre information from other agencies.
- Clear procedures for enquiries and referrals.
- Policies concerning invitations to other agencies to attend a centre's review of work with individual families and reviews of overall work.
- Policies relating to centre staff's attendance at case conferences or other agencies' reviews of work.
- Avenues for clarifying inter-agency difficulties or resolving conflicts.

Centres need to ensure that information is current and is regularly circulated. Staff in other agencies may leave and centres may also change their practice and procedures.

Barriers to effective collaboration between agencies

There are both organisational and individual barriers to positive inter-disciplinary collaboration. Organisational barriers include:

- different catchment areas for different agencies;
- competition between agencies for resources;
- disparate organisational structures;
- frequent restructuring of organisations.

Individual obstacles encompass:

- dissimilar training and backgrounds;
- varied philosophy and attitudes;
- different status and role.

Other major barriers to inter-agency cooperation are differences in goals, priorities and client groups. Thus a centre's goal in Garbarino's (1982) terminology may be the 'optimisation of opportunities' whilst an agency such as social services may be concentrating on the 'minimisation of risk'. Equally, a family centre's priority may be families with children under five – a priority which may be shared with health visitors but not with the local social workers or the housing department.

Conversely, a centre's primary focus may be families with children at risk and this may be shared with local social workers but not local schools.

Effective collaboration requires an acknowledgement and recognition of the many differences outlined. Differences need to be clarified and understood. But at the same time common and shared purposes and concerns need to be identified and emphasised. As Mumford (1986) states, 'fundamental to the development of any meaningful working relationship is everyone's commitment to the same objective'.

Formal and informal networks

Hasler (1984) suggests that one significant difference between family centres is the way that they operate in relation to both formal and informal systems. Thus he argues that a centre clearly working within the formal system of care 'will find itself acting much as a statutory department, but perhaps playing a specialised role'. Other centres, he suggests, are primarily concerned with the informal system of social networks and community groups. A third position is propounded – that of 'working across the boundary' where centres help people across the boundaries between formal and informal systems. A neighbourhood centre operating an integrated family centre model is likely to find itself in this third position where it is concerned to forge effective relationships with both formal and informal systems of care.

Whilst the importance of both formal and informal networks is emphasised in any report on social or community care, the relationship between them involves tension. Many family centres will experience this tension as they seek to collaborate with both systems. The informal networks are often suspicious and anxious in relation to the formal systems, fearing the possibilities of either interference or exploitation. Members of formal networks sometimes undervalue the contribution of the informal system or question its efficacy or quality. If family centres bridge both systems they may find participants expressing opposition to staff forming close working relationships with statutory agencies or, conversely, professional representatives of the formal systems doubting the judgement of centre staff about the contribution of local informal networks.

It is important that a centre reflects on its relation to the informal and formal systems. There can be a danger that a voluntary centre overemphasises its separation from the formal system; if it employs professional workers, who inevitably carry some degree of child-protection responsibilities, this is inaccurate. This distortion can also encourage participants in an unhelpful splitting of agencies into the 'bad' statutory services and the 'good' family centre. On the other hand, centres may concentrate fiercely on ensuring that they are accepted by and enmeshed into the formal system to the extent that they are alienated from the informal networks.

Bridging the formal and informal systems may be a very important and effective approach for family centres. The contribution of both systems is undeniably essential but differences between the networks makes their cooperation hazardous. A centre's link with both networks can enable staff and participants to encourage more productive and mutually beneficial relationships between formal and informal systems of care.

10

Issues and Challenges for Family Centres

Introduction

This chapter will explore a number of key challenges and issues which face family centres. It is inevitably selective as the very scope of this book indicates the range of concerns which a family centre needs to address.

Who are family centres for?

Selectivity issues

An increasing expectation of family centres is that they should fulfil a role in child protection and be a major part of a local authority's provision of services for children in need and their families. They are frequently viewed as a significant resource in maintaining children in their own families or in returning children home after separation. Such a focus will tend to be fulfilled by working with a selected group of families. The targeting of particular families may be justified by funders on the basis of the cost of the resource and the necessity of ensuring that it is used by families in greatest need. But arguments can be made for family centre services being available to a whole neighbourhood both from the ecological perspective explored earlier and on the basis that families 'with problems' should not be isolated from the rest of the community.

Some writers express concern about the impact of centres

working both with targeted families and the wider community. Thus Cannan (1986) writes:

> it could be that one of the shortcomings in family centre work is a tendency to gloss over the differences between 'problem families' and 'normal' but poor families . . . A service which may indeed help problem families may be inappropriate for other poor families, even undermining their neighbourhood.

Such a perspective, whilst rightly highlighting the dangers of stigmatisation, erroneously suggests that families fall into distinct categories between which the differences are greater than the similarities. The detrimental impact of such an approach is identified by Gill (1987) who points out that welfare provision 'often has the effect of pushing people apart. The consequence of the privatisation of social ills is that families are selected as different and then cut off from neighbours.' He urges a counter-approach, 'One of the key responsibilities of family centres working in local neighbourhoods must be to bring people together rather than push them apart.' Cannan (1992) herself, in a later publication, supports such an approach by promoting a model of family centre which provides a range of services and encourages variety in types of user.

Targeting particular families can also suggest that the sole source of their difficulties is found within the family. An ecological approach, as indicated earlier, would understand difficulties as arising from a complex interaction of factors, only some of which are located within a family. Such a view is supported by statistics demonstrating the disproportionate numbers of children entering care from poor families and from disadvantaged areas (Bebbington and Miles, 1989).

Analyses of child abuse which challenge explanations focusing solely on parental attributes or family processes are provided by Gil (1970) and (1979) and Parton (1985). Both writers emphasise the social and structural factors which contribute to child abuse.

Race issues

In common with other social-welfare provision, the respon-
siveness of family centres to families and communities of
minority ethnic groups can often be questioned. As part of the
wider social services, family centres are inevitably affected by
institutional racism. The Social Services Inspectorate's survey
of family centres (1988) commented that, 'some staff lacked
confidence in handling racist issues and this limited their
ability to provide an ethnic-sensitive service'.

Warren (1990) concluded from his survey of family centres
that they were, 'predominantly a service for white women'. A
few centres may be established to meet the specific needs of
particular minority ethnic groups. Thus De'Ath (1985) describes the Shree Ram Krishna Centre which:

> hopes to bring small groups of two or three mothers together in
> one home, to introduce them to each other and to encourage them
> to develop enough self-esteem and self-confidence to move from
> the home to meet with other mothers and join groups set up at the
> Centre in their Hindu temple.

There is evidence of some centres seeking to make services
accessible to minority ethnic groups. Thus Shinman (1988)
mentions the Soho Family Centre's Health Education groups
which are run in Bengali, Chinese and English. However,
such examples stand out in the literature, highlighting a lack
of serious attention to issues of race.

Whatever population a centre serves, anti-racist practice is
essential as all centres exist in a wider multi-ethnic and racist
society. Any anti-discriminatory practice improves the quality
of all service provision. Thus all family centres need to address
issues of racism, as Walker (1991) urges:

> If family centres are to continue to develop useful services it is
> essential that the work takes on an overtly anti-racist approach
> that goes deeper than the provision of multicultural toys and the
> celebrations of festivals, to a real understanding of the past and
> present experiences and concerns of black families.

This requires an understanding of the effects of racism on black and white, children and parents. It demands an honest examination of attitudes, values, assumptions and perceptions. An anti-racist approach means, for example, that language, procedures, images projected, routines and systems are all scrutinised to ensure that they are neither intentionally nor unintentionally racist. Centres may be assisted in developing an anti-racist approach by formulating a statement of intent and a detailed strategy for its implementation. One small but effective contribution to such a strategy is the inclusion of an item 'race issues' on every staff meeting agenda which can ensure that race issues are not marginalised but are a central, regular and integrated concern.

An anti-racist approach is one that has to be pursued in partnership with participants. This may involve debates, conflict and sometimes opposition. For example, efforts to ensure actively that the centre is accessible and sensitive to black users may be resisted by existing white users who fear they will lose services rather than see an improved quality in provision. Challenging racism overtly expressed by colleagues or centre users requires confidence and skill if it is to be successful. Role-plays of racist conversations or incidents already experienced by staff can develop strategies and confidence for tackling similar occasions in the future.

Gender issues

As already indicated, family centres tend to work predominantly with mothers. Kirk (1990) reporting on a Tayside survey states:

> Although the study did involve interviewing some fathers, there was little evidence of men using the facilities of family centres. The predominance of their work is with women, but this seemed neither acknowledged explicitly in policy nor were the implications for practice addressed.

A number of interrelated factors influence this gender imbalance. Family centres need to reflect on their approach to gender issues; recognising that it is a complex area. It would seem that most family centres share a wider social policy and public welfare attitude to gender and child care. The social construction of mothers as primarily responsible for children affects parents, referrers and family centre staff. Staff, other agencies and centre participants may unwittingly perpetuate the traditional expectations that involvement with welfare services is the responsibility of mothers.

Walker (1991) challenges this:

> Family centres need to consider what role they play in reinforcing gender inequalities and the implications of this for adults and children who use them. Does the centre implicitly accept that in most families mothers care for the children and focus their attention on women? Or should the centre challenge that assumption and insist on the active involvement of men and, if so, on what terms?

There are different cultural and class patterns in terms of family responsibilities and the relationships between women and men. For some minority ethnic groups, the involvement of men in a centre would preclude the attendance of women. Centre staff need to recognise that they may hold different expectations from centre participants about how child care and domestic tasks could or should be allocated between parents.

Individual families have different structures and patterns. A large proportion of female-headed lone-parent households in a neighbourhood will inevitably lead to greater use of a centre by women rather than men.

Most centres carry some focus on parenting and will work with an explicit or implicit concept of 'good enough' parenting. Hanmer and Statham (1988, p. 55) warn:

> But the way 'good enough' parenting is conceptualised minimises the recognition of the impact of the interaction of racism, sexism and social class on the social development of the child.

They also suggest that a concept of 'fit mother' operates in social work but that social workers do not use any equivalent 'fit father' role in their child care work. Ong (1986) emphasises the importance of professionals examining their attitudes and beliefs about motherhood and highlights the economic, social and psychological pressures on mothers.

The frequent equating of parent or parenting with mother or mothering not only places unreasonable demands and unjust pressures on women, it also leads to disadvantages for men and for children. It excludes men from the fulfilment and rewards of actively sharing in the care of their children and it denies opportunities to children.

On first consideration it may seem clear that family centres should be criticised for:

> reinforcing traditional roles for women as dependants and prime homemakers, while denying men opportunities to develop their parenting abilities and assume more responsibility for the care of their children (Kirk, 1990).

However, other writers caution that a greater involvement of fathers in child care does not automatically provide advantages for women. Oakley's research suggests that participation by fathers in child care was often restricted to the more pleasurable aspects and as she comments:

> This kind of enlargement in the father's role is an unfortunate development for women, who stand to gain little from it but temporary peace to do household chores . . . At the same time, they lose some of the rewards parenthood offers (Oakley, 1974, p. 180).

Leonard and Speakman (1986) point out that women hold such restricted power in the wider sphere that sharing parenting can result in a removal of the little power they have as primary parents:

> Altering the sexual division of labour and power within the family can thus actually be disadvantageous to women when the gender-related power relations outside the family remain unchanged (Leonard and Speakman, 1986, pp. 56–7).

A recognition of this danger challenges centres to play a role in seeking to change wider attitudes towards child care and opportunities for women. The paramountcy of children receiving quality care must be emphasised by centres so that parenthood is appropriately valued and the provision of child care afforded due status.

Women using family centres may have had limited educational and training possibilities. They may have become mothers at an early age. In a context of little hope of employment, motherhood may be perceived by young women as the sole affirmation of achieving adult status. Cannan (1992) points out that centres:

> should articulate with labour markets and the training system and provide opportunities for women, both through adult education and counselling within the centres and by providing day care to enable them to become independent and fulfilled.

However, when employment is available it rarely fits easily with the needs of children. As David (1985) points out, what is needed is a transformation in the organisation of work to accommodate the needs of children and parents:

> Such changes would provide more public and social support for all parents – mothers or fathers – and create a more supportive, social environment for the rearing of all children. They would enable men and women to make a public and private commitment to their children, free from both economic and emotional constraints.

Family centres may be able to do little towards such a major transformation; however staff can seek to ensure that issues of gender are recognised and confronted in all aspects of a centre's work.

Clarity about gender issues should be demonstrated in the referral and admission policy and in the allocation of work. Clearly the latter aspect is only an option where a mixed staff team exists, but exploration of the issues indicate the value of a team including women and men. In reaching decisions as to whether gender is a significant factor in work allocation a number of factors need to be considered.

First, the user's preference, feelings and experience are important. Thus many women who have been sexually abused may find it impossible to confide in a male worker. However, another woman may not find this problematic. Second, the feelings and experience of the worker have to be acknowledged. Thus some male workers may feel uncomfortable and unskilled in working with women or children who have suffered abuse from men. The aim and focus of the work form a third important factor to be taken into account. Where gender issues are central to the work – for example, a consciousness-raising group for women – it is essential that the groupworkers are women.

Frequently in family centres male workers will be working with women:

> men who work with women clients must own the negative aspects of their own power . . . Men, not just women, have to own up to their own feelings, thoughts and actions if there is to be gender sensitive practice and policy (Hanmer and Statham, 1988, pp. 118–19).

Work with men requires centre staff to examine their attitudes and skills. Holt (1992) explores the problems and possibilities of developing effective work with men within family centres.

A family centre team consisting of both women and men offers opportunities for working in non-sexist ways which share power and in which women and men intentionally fulfil roles traditionally associated with the other gender.

Disability issues

The approach of the Children Act (1989) integrates services for children with a disability with those provided for other children 'in need'. This challenges family centres to examine how accessible and appropriate their services and activities are for children with a disability. Similarly they should consider parents with a disability. Family centres usually acknowledge the enormous demands of parenting but may not pay sufficient attention to the additional burden caused by the disability of either parent or child. In describing the KIDS

Family Centre, which offers a range of services to families who have a child with special needs, Pugh (1987) points out that 'the problems facing the families of handicapped children are likely to be both more acute and more diverse' than the needs of parents in general.

All too often, in common with other public services, the building, environment and ethos of a family centre presents people with a disability with unassailable obstacles and discouragement. Centres therefore have to address the needs of children or parents with a disability in terms of both the physical and psychological accessibility of their centre.

There is always a danger of assuming that services are sensitive to people with disabilities when a building affords wheelchair access. The issues are of course immensely wider than this and disability arises from a range of illnesses and impairments. It is well-documented how physical and psychological effects are compounded by prejudice and discrimination. Increasingly centres will be offering services to children and/or parents with Aids or HIV. This raises issues of awareness and training for staff and for participants as any such service has to battle with existing ignorance, prejudice and neglect.

Parents and children together

Many of the challenges facing family centres relate to working with both children and parents.

Children's needs or parents' needs

Walker (1991) echoes the experience of most family centre workers when she comments 'In family centre practice a balance between parents and children is often very difficult to achieve.'

It can be argued that the development of family centres has of itself decreased the already scant resources provided to meet parents', and in particular, mothers' needs. The thrust towards family centres has led in several areas to a transformation of day nurseries into family centres and a resultant loss of day-care provision. Insistence on parental involvement can lead to a loss of services for parents. The effect of such a policy is felt by mothers who, as already indicated, still carry the greatest share of child care.

Various different attitudes may be taken by a family centre towards parents' needs, as outlined below:

Children are the responsibility of their parents and family centres should meet parents' needs to support them in their task.

If centres are for 'families' then each family-member's needs are a legitimate focus for a centre's activities. Adult members of a family should have their needs recognised as individuals and not solely in terms of their role as parent.

Family centres are concerned with each family-member's needs but the child's welfare must be paramount.

Children are the primary focus of family centres but as parents are their main carers their needs may have to be addressed if the children are to benefit.

Children are the primary focus of family centres and parents must be involved in order to meet their children's needs.

The balance which a centre strikes between parents' and children's needs will vary according to which of the above attitudes they espouse. It is important that a centre is clear about its perspective and philosophy and that this is understood by families and other agencies.

Parents' needs are many and varied and should be assessed jointly with the parents. Whilst parents may often feel their needs as adults are neglected by family centres they are, at least to some extent, able to articulate their need, whereas children, particularly young children, are not able to verbalise their needs.

As explored in Chapter 6 it is essential that family centres have a child perspective and consistently advocate for children's needs within the centre as well as beyond. Concern for both children and parents will sometimes result in conflict. Many incidents and events will enable a centre to explore with its users the tensions between parents' needs and children's needs.

Example 10.1

Money was donated to Fulford Family Centre for children of lone parents and a lively debate was held as to how it should be spent. Some parents were arguing for some of it to be used for social evenings for parents with a stated assumption that the parents enjoying a good night out would benefit the children. One parent retorted indignantly, 'If I have a good night out, it doesn't make me a better parent. It just makes me grumpy with them when I wake up the next morning.'

One way of managing the tension between children's needs and parent's needs in work with some individual families is to allocate two workers to the family – one worker focusing on the child's needs and the other on those of the parents. Whilst demanding of staff resources it is also very effective but it requires good communication and understanding between the workers involved, as inevitably the conflict and tension between the family members' needs may come to be experienced between the workers.

Protection and partnership

A further challenge to family centres which is closely allied to the tension between children's needs and parent's needs is the issue of child protection and partnership with parents. Some writers suggest that partnership and child protection are incompatible. Thus Pugh and De'Ath (1989, p. 72) write:

> Child protection and preventive work is based on an assumption that some parents cannot cope. The policing of care and contractual obligations are not conducive to partnership.

It is confusing to find protection and prevention subsumed in the same statement; the assumption must be made that preventive work here is being restricted to the prevention of neglect or abuse. The argument can be challenged for both types of work, for the assumption is surely not that some parents cannot *cope* but that they cannot cope *alone* and as outlined earlier this is an underlying philosophy of the Children Act 1989.

Some of the obstacles are more readily overcome when workers first recall the primary significance of parents in any child's life; and second, recognise that the vast majority of parents care for their children and desire their best interest, although different understanding about children's needs and enormous stress experienced by parents may obscure these facts. As Packman and Jordan (1991) state, when outlining aspects of the Cleveland Report:

> Even parents who were suspected of abuse retained a sense of responsibility for their children which should be nurtured, not crushed; and even the implementation of legal powers required respect, communication, the willingness to listen, and the desire to reach agreements – not least with the victims themselves.

Clearly partnership and protection may be incompatible if a decision is made that the only way to protect a particular child adequately is permanent removal from their parental care or where a parent indicates that they do not wish to fulfil their parental responsibility. But in other circumstances it is possible, and in fact the Children Act demands, that ways are found to pursue both child protection and partnership. As suggested in the previous section one approach which assists this extraordinarily difficult and demanding duality is the involvement of two workers with a family.

Staff and families together

The centre as a family

A family centre may itself be likened to a family; it can offer nurturing opportunities for development and enriching experiences but also like a family it can provide an arena for distress and impairment. Family centre staff can easily overlook the importance of a centre to its participants and its role as their extended family. Two Fulford Family Centre (1991) parents commented:

> There's never been support from my own family, the family centre filled that gap.

> If I hadn't gone to the centre I'd have been much more isolated and less able to cope. The family centre took over the role of uncles and aunts. My own family were not there.

Using the notion of family can be a simple and helpful framework in making sense of some of the processes and dynamics which emerge in a family centre. Staff may find themselves moving between roles with the same or different parents. At times they will be supporting the parent in the care of their child and the interaction will seem like two adults focusing on the child. On other occasions staff may feel that a parent is seeking nurturing and support for themselves and the interaction may feel like an adult (member of staff) responding to two children (the parent and the child.) Such interactions can be understood through various models. Psychodynamic approaches identify the presence and power of the inner infant or child. As indicated earlier one model which extends and applies this insight in a clear framework is transactional analysis.

Parents who participate in family centres may have received inadequate parenting themselves. They may require 're-parenting' by staff (and/or other parents) to enable them to internalise nurturing parental models. It is only when such internal models are available that parents can look after themselves and their children sufficiently well. Such staff/ parent interactions will often generate feelings and expressions of dependency by parents. Centre staff come to recognise that this is a process which is not to be avoided, but one which they need to work through with some parents to enable the parents to achieve essential 'growth'.

Roles and role strain

The wide range of activities undertaken in many family centres involves both staff and users in a complex matrix of roles. There seem to be both advantages and disadvantages of this matrix of roles.

A major advantage of multiple roles and relationships is the opportunity they afford staff and users to get to know one another in a broader and deeper way. Meeting the same person in different roles leads to the building up of a truer picture of the individual so that increasingly it is the person rather than the role which is experienced. Involvement in a wide range of activities with the same parent enables staff to be aware of strengths as well as difficulties. It also allows the possibility for a more equal relationship to develop and can reduce the likelihood of services/activities being stigmatised. Multiple roles for staff also contribute to an interesting, challenging and varied job.

Some roles are very similar and movement between them presents no problems for the role-holders, but between others movement seem quite difficult. Brown and Clough (1989) write:

> One of the most difficult aspects of life in day and residential centres for both staff and users is coping with all the changes and adaptations involved in moving from one group or grouping to another during the course of a day or a week.

There are then disadvantages in moving between different roles. One difficulty is that the number and variety of activities at a centre can lead to the place feeling 'too hectic' or 'chaotic'. Sometimes the number and breadth of roles carried by the same staff or parent may feel too great and this may be particularly apparent when varied activities are undertaken within the same day.

Undertaking certain roles may discourage a parent from seeking other roles. For instance, it may sometimes be difficult for a parent to seek counselling or similar services if they have become very active as a committee member or volunteer, as the parent may then feel the need to maintain a 'competent' appearance.

The movement between roles by the same worker and parent seems to be most demanding when one of the activities is counselling or 'confidential work'. It can be difficult for a parent who has just revealed distress in an individual session to see that member of staff immediately engage in light-hearted discussion with other parents. An additional implication may be that if a parent is feeling particularly stressed s/he may want to bring up issues, usually confined to his/her confidential session, during a different activity such as a committee meeting or an informal group.

It is interesting to explore what underlies this problem. In considering the difficulties identified in moving between counselling and other activities, it would appear that one of the roots of the problem lies in moving from an exclusive individual relationship with the worker to a shared group relationship. The complexities can therefore be defined in terms of managing boundaries. The strain of moving between roles is lessened for participants and staff when, first, thought is given to timetabling so that vastly different roles do not follow on from each other and second, by emphasising the boundaries through indicating the differences in activities and roles. Finally, ground-rules may need to be established between workers and individuals or groups as to how to manage particular overlaps which are proving stressful.

Relationships between workers and families

The chapter on partnership with parents explored many aspects of the relationship between staff and parents. Family centres, compared with many other social service settings, are places where it is possible for staff to be 'alongside' families. They often have the benefit of sharing in both the joys and sorrows of family life. As research such as Daines *et al.* (1990) has shown, parents often view staff as friends. This appears to be a tribute to workers' accessibility and style. As the same writers emphasise, friendliness on the part of staff is not the same as friendship and indicates appropriate involvement rather than over-involvement. For some, these issues relate to professionalism and what it means. The word is sometimes used pejoratively to describe remoteness and unhelpful detachment whilst in other contexts it denotes a quality of service. Most staff will be eager to pursue the latter and friendliness is not excluded from such an approach. Workers need to establish appropriate boundaries in their work with families, for boundaries protect centre participants. Boundaries can be distinguished from barriers which are usually erected to protect workers and are unhelpful to families.

Family centre staff may sometimes find themselves unwittingly behaving in a way which is more akin to the unhelpful image of a remote and clinically detached professionalism. It is important to explore possible reasons for such behaviour in order that it can be changed. It would seem that a remote professional stance is sometimes a defence against various sources of anxiety or depression. Contributing factors may be:

- the workers' fear of loss of privacy or autonomy which an over-emphasis on partnership may provoke;
- the workers' desire for protection from the overwhelming demands of the task in which they are engaged;
- the workers' avoidance of feelings of futility and despair in the face of disadvantage, poverty and distress which they are powerless to change.

Recognition of the painful reality with which both workers and users are frequently engaged can prevent workers retreating unhelpfully into a remote professionalism.

Pointers for wider social welfare provision

The work of family centres may generate or confirm some insights useful to wider social welfare provision. Certain writers even go so far as to suggest that 'the development of family centres, in all their variety, could play an important part in the movement towards the restructuring of social welfare services' (Willmott and Mayne, 1983, p. 146). This final section, then, briefly emphasises issues raised earlier in this book which appear to have application to other welfare provision. The comments relate primarily to centres using what was referred to earlier as an integrated model. Yet most centres will share to some degree the features outlined below; many of them are closely related.

Collectivity and connection

Family centres can facilitate the sharing of concerns and resources between families. The traditional approach of most social services' provision has been to focus on individuals and their families. It is uncommon for groupworkers or community workers to find their methods enthusiastically encouraged by organisations. Family centres apply and confirm the wisdom of groupwork and community work; that bringing people together enables the discovery of collective solutions. It also affirms and strengthens people.

Combating stigma

An unintentional result of much welfare provision is stigmatisation. Family centres can recognise the stress of child care and family life for all families and challenge perspectives which seek to divide families into 'copers' and 'non-copers'; 'successes' and 'failures'; 'normal families' and 'problem families'.

Ecological or holistic approach

A feature of the family centre movement has been its espousal of an ecological or holistic approach. It has emphasised the importance of looking at the whole person in his/her particular context and environment. Centres seek an understanding of the interconnected elements of each family's possibilities and predicaments. In addition they attempt to address those opportunities and risks in multiple and varied ways.

Participation and empowerment

It is now recognised that, in addition to stigmatising, social services often disempower. Participation and empowerment are increasingly popular words in articles and books but practice is often slow to follow philosophy. It appears that family centres are genuinely struggling with these issues and their implications, and family centre conferences form one of the few arenas where professional workers and 'clients' or 'consumers' meet and work together.

Formal and informal networks

Family centres indicate the value of both forms of network and the importance of their being linked. Many of the traditional features of social services' organisation and practice militate against a close connection with informal networks. Thus the individualisation of problems, the lack of groupwork and community work, the stigmatisation of 'clients', bureaucratic and hierarchical structures provide formidable obstacles for staff intent on working with informal networks. Conversely, many of the characteristics of family centres facilitate relationships being forged with informal networks.

Implications for workers, volunteers and students

As in most day and residential provision, a family centre's staff, volunteers and students operate in a 'public arena'. Their style and work are constantly observed by participants and colleagues. This can offer considerable opportunities for learning and development and assists in the maintenance of standards of service. But it can also be a source of anxiety and discomfort. Maximising the opportunities afforded requires a climate of positive feedback and constructive criticism. Pursuit of many of the factors identified in this chapter requires workers who demonstrate an openness in their practice. This includes a readiness to be challenged by families and colleagues.

Evaluating effectiveness

In common with much social welfare provision, there is an absence of both quantitative and qualitative evaluation of family centres. Both participants and workers are enthusiastic advocates for the existence and development of family centres. Such advocacy provides clear testimony to the benefits of family centres. However, further research and evaluation is needed to compare different models and to provide detailed evidence about the particular value and effectiveness of family centres.

Bibliography

Adams, Robert (1990) *Self-help, Social Work and Empowerment*, Basingstoke, Macmillan/BASW.

Adamson, Joy and Warren, Chris (1983) *Welcome to St Gabriel's Family Centre!*, London, The Children's Society.

Ahmad, Bandana (1990) *Black Perspectives in Social Work*, Birmingham, Venture Press.

Ahmed, S., Cheetham, J., and Small, J. (1987) *Social Work with Black Children and their Families*, London, Batsford.

Allan, Graham (1985) *Family Life*, Oxford, Basil Blackwell.

Arnstein, R.A. (1972) 'Power to the People: An Assessment of the Community Action and Model Cities Experience', *Public Administration Review*, vol.32.

Bainham, Andrew (1990) 'The Children Act 1989: The State and the Family', *Family Law*, June, pp. 231–4.

Balbo, Laura (1987) 'Crazy Quilts: Rethinking the Welfare State Debate from a Woman's Point of View', in Anne Showstack Sassoon (ed.) *Women and the State*, London, Hutchinson.

Ballard, Roger (1982) 'South-Asian Families', in R.N. Rapoport, M.P. Fogarty and R. Rapoport (eds) *Families in Britain*, London, Routledge & Kegan Paul.

Barclay Report (1982) *Social Workers: Their Roles and Tasks*, London, Bedford Square Press and NCVO.

Barrow, Jocelyn (1982) 'West Indian Families: An Insider's Perspective', in R.N. Rapoport, M.P. Fogarty and R. Rapoport (eds) *Families in Britain*, London, Routledge & Kegan Paul.

Bebbington, Andrew and Miles, John (1989) 'The Background of Children who enter Local Authority Care', *British Journal of Social Work*, 19, pp. 349–68.

Begum, Nasa (1991) 'Setting the Context: Disability and the Children Act 1989', in Macdonald (1991).

Berne, Eric (1967) *Games People Play*, London, Penguin.

Bowlby, John (1979) *The Making and Breaking of Affectional Bonds*, London, Tavistock.

Bowlby, John (1980) *Attachment and Loss, vol. 3: Loss, Sadness and Depression*, London, Hogarth.

Bronfenbrenner, U. (1979) *The Ecology of Human Development: Experiments by Nature and Design*, Cambridge, Massachusetts, Harvard University Press.

Brown, Allan (1992) *Groupwork*, 3rd edn, Aldershot, Gower.

Brown, Allan, and Clough, Roger (1989) *Groups and Groupings: Life and Work in Day and Residential Centres*, London, Tavistock/ Routledge.

Brown, George and Harris, Tirrell (1978) *Social Origins of Depression: A Study of Psychiatric Disorder in Women*, London, Tavistock.

Browne, Naima and France, Pauline (1986) '"Unclouded Minds Saw Unclouded Visions": Visual Images in the Nursery', in Naima Browne and Pauline France (eds) *Untying the Apron Strings: Anti-sexist Provision for the Under-Fives*, Milton Keynes, Open University Press.

Bryan, Agnes (1992) 'Working with Black Single Mothers: Myths and Reality', in Mary Langan and Lesley Day (eds) *Women, Oppression and Social Work: Issues in Anti-Discriminatory Practice*, London, Routledge.

Buckinghamshire County Council, Social Services Department (1987) *Family Centres in Buckinghamshire, Report of Review of Children's Services Implementation Group*.

Butler, Barbara and Elliott, Doreen (1985) *Teaching and Learning for Practice*, Aldershot, Gower.

Calvert, Jane (1985) 'Motherhood', in Eve Brook and Ann Davis (eds) *Women, the Family and Social Work*, London, Tavistock.

Cannan, Crescy (1986) 'Sanctuary or Stigma', *Community Care*, 22 May, pp. 14–17.

Cannan, Crescy (1992) *Changing Families Changing Welfare: Family Centres and the Welfare State*, Hemel Hempstead, Harvester Wheatsheaf.

Cigno, Katy (1987) *Clacton Family Project: A Study*, London, Save the Children.

Cigno, Katy (1988) 'Consumer Views of a Family Centre Drop-In', *British Journal of Social Work*, 18, pp. 361–75.

Coit, K (1978) 'Local Action not Citizen Participation', in W. Tabb and L. Sawers (eds) *Marxism and the Metropolis*, New York, Oxford University Press.

Committee on Child Health Services (1976) *Fit for the Future* (Court Report).

Coussins, Jean, and Coote, Anna (1981) *The Family in the Firing Line*,

London, Child Poverty Action Group and National Council for Civil Liberties.

Cox, David, and Parish, Amanda (1989) *Working in Partnership Themes and Issues*, City of Birmingham Polytechnic and Barnardo's.

Croft, Suzy, and Beresford, Peter (1991) 'Giving is Better than You Get', *Social Work Today*, 3 October.

Daines, Rene, Lyons, Kate, and Parsloe, Phyllida (1990) *Aiming for Partnership*, Ilford, Barnardo's.

Dale, Peter (1991) 'Dangerous Families Revisited', *Community Care*, 14 November, pp. 14–15.

Dale, Peter, Davies, Murray, Morrison, Tony and Waters, Jim (1986) *Dangerous Families: Assessment and Treatment of Child Abuse*, London, Tavistock.

David, Miriam (1985) 'Motherhood and Social Policy a Matter of Education?', *Critical Social Policy*, issue 12, vol. 4, no. 3, pp. 28–43.

David, Miriam (1991) 'Putting on an Act for Children', in Mavis Maclean and Dulcie Groves (eds) *Women's Issues in Social Policy*, London, Routledge.

De'Ath, Erica (1985) *Self-Help and Family Centres: A Current Initiative in Helping the Community*, London, National Children's Bureau.

Department of Education and Science (1967) *Children and their Primary Schools, Report of the Central Advisory Council for Education (England)*, (Plowden Report), London, HMSO.

Department of Education and Science and Welsh Office (1977) *A New Partnership for our Schools* (Taylor Report), London, HMSO.

Department of Education (1978) *Report of the Enquiry into the Education of Handicapped Children and Young People: Special Educational Needs*, (Warnock Report), London, HMSO.

Department of Health (1988) *Protecting Children: A Guide for Social Workers Undertaking a Comprehensive Assessment*, London, HMSO.

Department of Health (1989) *An Introduction to the Children Act 1989*, London, HMSO.

Department of Health (1991a) *The Children Act 1989: Guidance and Regulations, Volume 1, Court Orders*, London, HMSO.

Department of Health (1991b) *The Children Act 1989: Guidance and Regulations, Volume 2, Family Support, Day Care and Educational Provision for Young Children*, London, HMSO.

Department of Health and Social Security (1985) *Social Work Decisions in Child Care*, London, HMSO.

DiPhillips, Netta and Elliott, Vicky (1987) 'The Amersham Family Centre', *Child Abuse Review*, Spring, 1 (5) pp. 13–16.

Dominelli, Lena (1988) *Anti-Racist Social Work*, Basingstoke, Macmillan.

Douglas, Tom (1976) *Groupwork Practice*, London, Tavistock.

Douglas, Tom (1978) *Basic Groupwork*, London, Tavistock.

Douglas, Tom (1983) *Groups*, London, Tavistock.

Douglas, Robin, and Payne, Chris (1988) *Organising for Learning. Staff Development Strategies for Residential and Day Services Work: A Theoretical and Practical Guide*, London, National Institute for Social Work.

Downie, Andrew, and Forshaw, Penny (1987) 'Family Centres', *Practice*, 2, pp. 140–7.

Driver, Geoffrey, (1982) 'West Indian Families : An Anthropological Perspective', in R.N. Rapoport, M.P. Fogarty and R. Rapoport (eds) *Families in Britain*, London, Routledge & Kegan Paul.

Drucker, Peter (1977) *People and Performance: The Best of Peter Drucker on Management*, London, Heinemann.

Eichenbaum, Luise and Orbach, Susie (1985) *Understanding Women*, Harmondsworth, Penguin.

Eisenstadt, Naomi (1986) 'Parental Involvement: Some Feminist Issues', inNaima Browne and Pauline France (eds) *Untying the Apron Strings: Anti-Sexist Provision for the Under-Fives*, Buckingham, Open University Press.

Fact Sheet 1, *The Family Today* (1991) Family Policy Studies Centre.

Fahlberg, Vera (1982) *Child Development*, London, British Agencies for Adoption and Fostering.

Ferri, Elsa, and Saunders, Anne (1991) *Parents, Professionals and Pre-school Centres: A Study of Barnardo's Provision*, London, Barnardo's and National Children's Bureau.

Fitzgerald, John, and Walsh, Kathy (1990) *Family Centres*, London, Bridge Child Care Consultancy.

Fox Harding, Lorraine (1991) *Perspectives in Child Care Policy*, London, Longman.

Franklin, Bob (ed.) (1986) *The Rights of Children*, Oxford, Blackwell.

Frost, Nick (1992) 'Implementing the Children Act 1989 in a Hostile Climate', in Pam Carter, Tony Jeffs and Mark K. Smith (eds) *Changing Social Work and Welfare*, Buckingham, Open University Press.

Fry, P.S. and Addington, J. (1984) '"Professionals" Negative Expectations of Boys from Father-headed Single-parent Families: Implications for Training of Child Care Professionals', *British Journal of Developmental Psychology*, 2, pp. 337–46.

Fulford Family Centre (1991) *Annual Report*.

Fuller, Roger and Stevenson, Olive (1983) *Policies, Programmes and*

Disadvantage: A Review of Literature, London, Heinemann.

Garbarino, James (1982) *Children and Families in the Social Environment*, New York, Aldine.

Gibbons, Jane (1990) *Family Support and Prevention: Studies in Local Areas*, London, HMSO.

Gil, David (1970) *Violence against Children*, Cambridge, Massachusetts, Harvard University Press.

Gil, David (1979) 'Unraveling Child Abuse', in Richard Bourne and Eli Newberger (eds), *Critical Perspectives on Child Abuse*, Massachussetts, Lexington Books.

Gill, Owen (1987) 'Love Thy Neighbourhood Family Centre', *Community Care*, 15 October, pp. 20–2.

Gill, Owen (1988) 'Integrated Work in a Neighbourhood Family Centre', *Practice* 2:3, pp. 243–55.

Gill, Owen (1992) *Parenting under Pressure: A Study of Forty Families Living in One Street*, Cardiff, Barnardo's.

Goldberg, Tina and Sinclair, Ian (1985) *Family Support Exercise*, London, National Institute for Social Work.

Goody, Esther and Groothues, Christine Muir (1979) 'Stress in Marriage', in Verity Saifullah Kahn (eds), *Minority Families in Britain*, Basingstoke, Macmillan.

Hallett, C. (1987) *Critical Issues in Participation*, Newcastle upon Tyne, Association of Community Workers.

Hallett, Christine (1989) *Women and Social Services Departments*, Hemel Hempstead,Harvester Wheatsheaf.

Handy, Charles (1988) *Understanding Voluntary Organisations*, Harmondsworth, Penguin.

Hanmer, Jalna, and Statham, Daphne (1988) *Women and Social Work: Towards a Woman-Centred Practice*, Basingstoke, Macmillan/BASW.

Hasler, Joe (1984) *Family Centres: Different Expressions, Same Principles*, London, Children's Society.

Heller, Robert (1972) *The Naked Manager*, London, Barrie & Jenkins.

Henderson, Paul, and Thomas, David (1989) *Skills in Neighbourhood Work*, London, Unwin Hyman.

Holman, Bob (1987) 'Family Centres', *Children and Society*, 2, pp. 157–73.

Holman, Bob (1988) *Putting Families First: Prevention and Child Care*, Basingstoke, Macmillan.

Holman, Bob (1992a) *Family Centres, Highlight No. 111*, London, National Children's Bureau and Barnardo's.

Holman, Bob (1992b) 'Linking up with the Locals', *Community Care*, 30 July pp. 14–15.

Holt, Colin (1992) *Developing Effective Work with Men within Family*

Centres, Personal Social Services, Fellowship Report, Bristol University.

Hudson, Annie (1989) 'Changing Perspectives: Feminism, Gender and Social Work', in Mary Langan and Phil Lee (eds) *Radical Social Work Today*, London, Unwin Hyman.

Hudson, B. (1989) 'Centers of Excellence', *Care Weekly*, no. 90, 21 July, pp. 12–13.

Ingleby Report (1960) *Report of the Committee on Children and Young Persons*, Cmnd 1191, HMSO.

James, M. and Jongeward, D. (1971) *Born to Win*, Reading, Massachusetts, Addison-Wesley.

Kahan, Barbara (1988) *Rye Hill: Working with Abused Children and their Families*, City of Newcastle upon Tyne.

Kirk, Ros (1990) 'Family Centres for the 90s', *Scottish Child*, Aug/Sept. pp. 10–11.

Kovel, Joel (1983) *A Complete Guide to Therapy from Psychoanalysis to Behaviour Modification*, Harmondsworth, Penguin.

Land, Hilary, and Parker, Roy (1978) 'United Kingdom', in Sheila Kamerman and Alfred Kahn (eds) *Family Policy Government and Families in Fourteen Countries*, New York, Columbia University Press.

Langan, Mary (1992) 'Who Cares? Women in the Mixed Economy of Care', in Mary Langan and Lesley Day (eds) *Women, Oppression and Social Work Issues in Anti-Discriminatory Practice*, London, Routledge.

Leissner, Aryeh (1967) *Family Advice Services*, London, Longmans.

Leonard, Diana, and Speakman, Mary Anne (1986) 'Women in the Family: Companions or Caretakers', in Veronica Beechey and Elizabeth Whitelegg (eds) *Women in Britain Today*, Buckingham, Open University Press.

Liffman, Michael (1978) *Power for the Poor: The Family Centre Project: An Experiment in Self-help*, Sydney, George Allen & Unwin.

Macdonald, Sheila (1991) *All Equal Under the Act?*, London, Race Equality Unit, NISW.

Manor, Oded (1991) 'Assessing the Work of a Family Centre: Services Offered and Referrers' Perceptions. A Pilot Study', *Journal of Family Therapy*, 13, pp. 285–94.

McCaughan, Nano (ed.) (1978) *Groupwork: Learning and Practice*, London, George Allen & Unwin.

McKechnie, Neil (1986a) 'Family Centres: A Shared Preventive Relationship with the Community', *Child Abuse Review*, 1 (3) Summer 1986, pp. 5–9.

McKechnie, Neil (1986b) 'Family Centres: Partnership with

Parents and Children in the Community', *Scottish Child*, no. 10, pp. 11–12.

McMahon, Linnet (1992) *The Handbook of Play Therapy*, London, Tavistock/Routledge.

Miller, Clive, and Scott, Tony (1984) *Strategies and Tactics: Planning and Decision Making in Social Services Fieldwork Teams*, London, National Institute for Social Work.

Mittler, Peter and Mittler, Helle (1983) 'Partnership with Parents: An Overview', in Peter Mittler and Helen McConachie (eds) *Parents, Professionals and Mentally Handicapped People: Approaches to Partnership*, Beckenham, Croom Helm.

Morgan, D.H.J. (1985) *The Family, Politics and Social Theory*, London, Routledge & Kegan Paul.

Mumford, D. (1986) 'Forging Positive Links', *Community Care*, 2 October, pp. 22–3.

Nelson-Jones, Richard (1982) *The Theory and Practice of Counselling*, London, Holt, Rinehart & Winston.

Oakley, Ann (1974) *The Sociology of Housework*, Oxford, Martin Robertson.

Oakley, Robin (1979) 'Family, Kinship and Patronage', in Verity Saifullah Kahn, *Minority Families in Britain*, Basingstoke, Macmillan.

Ong, Bie Nio (1986) 'Child Abuse: Are Abusing Women Abused Women?' in Christine Webb (ed.) *Feminist Practice in Women's Health Care*, Chichester, John Wiley.

Packman, Jean, and Jordan, Bill (1991) 'The Children Act: Looking Forward, Looking Backward', *British Journal of Social Work*, 21 pp. 315–27.

Parker, Roy A. (1980) *Caring for Separated Children*, Basingstoke, Macmillan.

Parker, Roy A. (1990) *Away from Home: A Short History of Provision for Separated Children*, Ilford, Barnardo's.

Parsloe, Phyllida (1981) *Social Services Area Teams*, London, George Allen & Unwin.

Parsons, Talcott (1970) *Social Structure and Personality*, New York, Free Press.

Parton, Nigel (1985) *The Politics of Child Abuse*, Basingstoke, Macmillan.

Payne, Chris, and Scott, Tony (1982) *Developing Supervision of Teams in Field and Residential Social Work*, London, National Institute for Social Work Papers, no 12.

Phelan, Jan (1983) *Family Centres: A Study*, London, The Children's Society.

Pitman, Elizabeth (1984) *Transactional Analysis for Social Workers and*

Counsellors, London, Tavistock/Routledge & Kegan Paul.

Pitman, Elizabeth (1990) *This Won't Change Your Life (But it Might Help!)*, Clevedon, Channel View Books.

Polansky, Norman, Gaudin, James, Ammons, Paul and Davis, Katheryn (1985) 'The Psychological Ecology of the Neglectful Mother', *Child Abuse and Neglect*, vol.9, pp. 265–75.

Preston-Shoot, Michael (1987) *Effective Groupwork*, Basingstoke, Macmillan/BASW.

Pringle, Mia Kellmer (1982) *Investment in Children*, Hugh Greenwood lecture, University of Exeter.

Pugh, Gillian (1987) 'KIDS Family Centre, Camden', in Gillian Pugh, Geoff Aplin, Erica De'Ath and Margaret Moxon, *Partnership in Action – Working with Parents in Pre-school Centres*, London, National Children's Bureau.

Pugh, Gillian (1988) *Services for Under Fives Developing a Coordinated Approach*, London, National Children's Bureau.

Pugh, Gillian, and De'Ath, Erica (1984) *The Needs of Parents: Practice and Policy in Parent Education*, Basingstoke, Macmillan.

Pugh, Gillian and De'Ath, Erica (1989) *Working towards Partnership in the Early Years*, London, National Children's Bureau.

Quinton, David, and Rutter, Michael (1988) *Parenting Breakdown: The Making and Breaking of Inter-generational Links*, Aldershot, Avebury.

Race Equality Unit/Black and White Alliance (1990) *Race in Child Protection*, London, Race Equality Unit, NISW.

Rapoport, Robert and Rapoport, Rhona (1982) 'British Families in Transition', in R.N. Rapoport, M.P. Fogarty and R. Rapoport (eds) *Families in Britain*, London, Routledge & Kegan Paul.

Reith, Drew (1979) 'A Family Assessment Guide', *Social Work Today*, vol. 10, no. 18, 2 January, pp. 18–19.

Report of the Committee on Local Authority and Allied Personal Social Services (1968) (Seebohm Report), London, HMSO, Cmnd 3703.

Rutter, Michael and Madge, Nicola (1976) *Cycles of Disadvantage: A Review of Research*, London, Heinemann.

Schaffer, H.R. (1988) 'Family Structure or Interpersonal Relationships: The Context for Child Development', *Children and Society*, 2, pp. 91–101.

Seebohm Report (1968) *see* Report of the Committee on Local Authority and Allied Personal Social Services.

Shaw, M.E. (1976) *Group Dynamics*, New York, McGraw-Hill.

Shinman, Sheila (1988) 'Soho Family Centre and its Contribution to Child Health', *Early Child Development and Care*, vol. 36, pp. 25–30.

Smith, Theresa (1987) 'Family Centres: Prevention, Partnership or

Community Alternative?' in j.A. Macfarlane, *Progress in Child Health*, vol. 3, pp. 176–89.

Social Services Inspectorate (1986) *Inspection of Family Centres – A National Survey of Family Centres Run by Local Authority Social Services Departments*, London, Department of Health and Social Security.

Social Services Inspectorate (1988) *Family Centres – A Change of Name or a Change of Practice*, London, Department of Health.

Specht, Harry, and Vickery, Anne (eds) (1977) *Integrating Social Work Methods*, London, Allen & Unwin.

Stewart, J.K., Yee, M.D. and Brown, R.J. (1990) 'Changing Social Work Roles in Family Centres: A Social Psychological Analysis', *British Journal of Social Work*, 20, pp. 45–64.

Stewart, John (1992) 'Guidelines for Public Service Management, Lessons not to be Learnt from the Private Sector', in Pam Carter, Tony Jeffs, and Mark K. Smith (eds) *Changing Social Work and Welfare*, Buckingham, Open University Press.

Stones, Christine (1989) 'Groups and Groupings in a Family Centre', in Allan Brown, and Roger Clough (eds) *Groups and Groupings*, London, Tavistock/Routledge.

Street, Eddy and Dryden, Windy (eds) (1988) *Family Therapy in Britain*, Milton Keynes, Open University Press.

Thamesdown's Voluntary Service Centre (1983) *Local Partnership in Action – A Look at Family Projects in Swindon*, Swindon, Thamesdown's Voluntary Service Centre.

Thorne, Barrie, and Yalom, Marilyn (eds) (1982) *Rethinking the Family*, New York, Longman.

Tibbenham, Alan (1986) 'The West Devon Family Centre: A Study of the Outcome of Work with Families between 1982–84', *Social Services Research*, vol. 15, no. 4 and 5, pp. 113–37.

Tristam, Stephanie (1986) 'Working in Partnership with Parents – Taking Account of Inhibiting Factors and Acknowledging Implications', *Scottish Child*, Summer 1986, p. 5.

Trowell, Judith, and Huffington, Clare (1992) 'Daring To Take A Risk: Issues from the First Year of the Monroe Young Family Centre', *ACPP Newsletter*, vol. 14, no 3, pp. 114–18.

Truax, Charles, and Carkhuff, Robert (1967) *Towards Effective Counselling and Psychotherapy*, Chicago, Aldine.

Turner, Christopher (1986) 'Family Structure and Behaviour in Britain since 1945', in G. Horobin (ed.) *Research Highlights in Social Work, 12 – The Family: Context or Client?*, London, Kogan Page.

Twelvetrees, Alan (1991) *Community Work*, 2nd edn, Basingstoke, Macmillan/BASW.

Walker, Hilary (1991) 'Family Centres', in Pam Carter, Tony Jeffs and Mark Smith (eds) *Social Work and Social Welfare Year Book 3*, Buckingham, Open University Press.

Warren, Chris (1986) 'Towards a Family Centre Movement: Reconciling Day Care, Child Protection and Community Work', *Child Abuse Review* 1 (3) Summer 1986.

Warren, Chris (1990) *The Potential for Parent Advocacy in Family Centres*, M.Phil. Thesis, University of Southampton.

Williams, Fiona (1992) '"The Family": Changes, Challenges and Contradictions', in Pam Carter, Tony Jeffs and Mark K. Smith (eds) *Changing Social Work and Welfare*, Buckingham, Open University Press.

Willmott, Phyllis, and Mayne, Susan (1983) *Families at the Centre*, London, Bedford Square Press/NCVO.

Wilson, Amrit (1978) *Finding a Voice: Asian Women in Britain*, London, Virago.

Wood, David, McMahon, Linnet and Cranstoun, Yvonne (1980) *Working with Under Fives*, London, Grant McIntyre.

Younghusband, Eileen (1978) *Social Work in Britain 1950–1975: A Follow-up Study*, London, Unwin.

Index

activities 62
Adams, R. 90–1
Adamson, J. 25
Addington, J. 4
advice work 62–8
advocacy 62–8, 105, 122, 168
Ahmad, B. 14
Ahmed, S. 58
aims and objectives 53, 136–9, 141, 142
Allan, G. 6
anti-discriminatory policy and practice xiv, 14, 54, 70, 104, 135–6, 145, 161–2, 163–7
anti-racism 52, 54, 109, 135, 145, 161–2
see also anti-discriminatory policy and practice
approaches 74–101
Arnstein, R. 127
assessment 57–8
of children 105–6
of parenting 57, 89, 115

Bainham, A. 13
Balbo, L. 16
Ballard, R 5
Banbury Family Centre 40
Barclay Report 24, 68, 71, 117, 144
Barnardo's viii, ix, 120
Barrow, J. 5
Bebbington, A. 160
Begum, N. 15
Beresford, P. 62

Berne, E. 83
Bowlby, J. 103
Bronfenbrenner, U. 9
Brown, A. 87, 88, 91, 127, 172
Brown, G. 7
Browne, N. 104
Bryan, A. 5
Buckinghamshire County Council 39
building 70
and children's needs 104–5
Butler, B. 60

Calvert, J. 7
Cannan, C. 17, 25, 27–8, 33, 36, 40–1, 43, 160, 165
Carkhuff, R. 77
catchment area 41–2, 138
categorisation of centres 31–3
Centres socio-culturels 28
child
abuse 13, 20–1, 30, 49, 78, 160
focus 42–4
paramountcy of welfare 116
perspective 102–16, 168
protection 12, 13, 20, 40, 48, 49, 58, 63, 80–1, 157, 159, 169–70
children
age of 38–9
in care 22, 31, 107, 120, 159, 160, 170
looked after by local authority 14, 38, 64, 70, 88, 107
in need 16, 25, 137, 138, 159

needs of 42–4, 102–5, 167–9
and parents 111–16, 167–9
rights of 12, 13, 14, 63–4, 102, 136
working with groups of 108–11
working with individual 105–8
Children Act (1948) 20
Children Act (1989) 13, 54
children with disabilities 15
children in need 16, 25, 137, 138
children's rights 102
children's wishes 63
family centres 24–5
family support 24, 27
partnership with parents 14, 103, 118, 170
race 14
registration 109
section 27 154
written agreements 55
Children and Young Persons Act (1963) 19, 20, 21
children's homes 22–3, 34, 46
see also family centre origins; residential care
Children's Society 25, 26, 27
Cigno, K. 17, 25
Cleveland Report 170
client-focused centres *see under* family centres
Clough, R. 87, 127, 172
Coit, K. 123
community
care 12, 22–3, 157
creating a profile of 95–6
development *see* community work
geographical 94–5
of interest 94–5
community development centres *see under* family centres
community work 93–101
confidentiality 73, 81
contact
between centre and families 55
between children and parents 70

contract
between centre and families 55–7
and service agreements 37, 57
Coote, A. 12
counselling 76–84, 172–3
couples, working with 84–6
Court Committee 118
Coussins, J. 12
Cox, D. 155
Croft, S. 62

Daines, R. 117, 118, 120, 126, 128, 132, 149, 173
Dale, P. 58
David, M. 16, 17, 165
day care 14, 16, 23–4, 38, 41, 42, 109, 114–15, 167–8
De'Ath, E. 7, 26, 31, 119, 126, 132, 161, 169
Department of Health 32, 58
Department of Health and Social Security 23, 26, 119
Department of Social Security 65, 66, 122
DiPhillips, N. 25
disability xiv, 15, 16, 25, 166–7
Dominelli, L. 5, 8
Douglas, R. 137, 138, 139
Douglas, T. 91
Downie, A. 25, 32
Driver, G. 5
Drucker, P. 133
Dryden, W. 84

ecological approach 9–10, 175
Eichenbaum, L. 8
Eisenstadt, N. 44
Elliott, D. 60
Elliott, V. 25
empowerment 62, 78, 126, 127–8, 135–6, 175
see also partnership with parents
ending *see* termination
equal opportunities 47, 145
see also race; anti-discriminatory policy and practice
equipment 70, 105, 108, 110

ethnic minorities *see* minority
ethnic groups
ethnic monitoring   54, 141–2
evaluation   58–9, 139–43, 176–7

Fahlberg, V.   106
families
  lone-parent   4, 5, 43, 79, 87,
    109, 139, 142, 163, 169
  working with   84–6, 111–14
family   1–17
  and environment   8–11
  and family centres   17–18
  myth and reality   2–8
  needs of members   7–8
  patterns   4–6
  policies   11–13
  rights   63–4
  roles   4–6
  and the state   11–17
  structure   3–4
  therapy   24, 84–6, 112
  and welfare services   15–17
Family Advice Centres   19, 21
Family Centre Network   xiii
family centres
  age of children   38–39
  catchment area   41–2
  categorisation   31–3
  client-focused model   27, 32,
    40–1, 43
  common factors   30–1
  community development
    model   27, 30, 32, 40–1
  context   37–8
  different dimensions   33–47
  evolution   19–28
  focus   42–4, 48
  funding sources   36–7, 48
  integrated model   49–51
  literature   25–8
  local authority   36–7, 39, 123,
    128, 135
  neighbourhood model   xiii, 27,
    32, 50
  origins   34–6
  philosophies   30
  precursors   19–20

  profiles   47–9
  referral to   39, 40, 48, 49, 53–4
  residential   45, 57
  role of users   45–6, 48
  self-help   26, 33, 36–7
  service model   33
  staffing   *see* staff
  target for intervention   40–1
  therapeutic   32, 40–1
  voluntary agency   25–7, 31,
    36–7, 123, 128, 154, 158
Family Policy Studies Centre   3
Family Service Units   19, 57
fathers   6, 8, 43–4, 47, 55, 89, 146,
    162–5
Ferri, E.   24
Fitzgerald, J.   153
Forshaw, P.   25, 32
Fox Harding, L.   12, 13
France   28
France, P.   104
Franklin, B.   63
Frost, N.   16
Fry, P.   4
Fulford Family Centre   xiii, 41,
    43, 66, 67, 68, 82, 93, 97, 101,
    110, 119, 120–2, 171
Fuller, R.   24
funding   36–7, 48

Garbarino, J.   6, 9, 10, 21, 30, 156
gender   4–8, 47, 103, 104, 145–6,
    162–6
Gibbons, J.   27
Gil, D.   160
Gill, O.   10, 25, 41, 43, 160
Gingerbread   34
goals   30, 48
Goldberg, T.   29
Goody, E.   5
Groothues, C. Muir   5
groups   86–93
  aims   87
  children's   108–11
  informal   90
  membership   88
  parenting   88–9
  parents and children   114–16

personal development 89–90
range of 87–91
self-help 90–1
groupwork 86–93, 148–50

Hallett, C. 17, 123
Handy, C. 133
Hanmer, J. 6, 8, 163, 166
Harris, T. 7
Hasler, J. 25, 31, 157
Heller, R. 133
Henderson, P. 95, 97, 143
Holman, B. 17, 25, 26–7, 28, 31, 32, 36, 40, 43, 123
Holt, C. 44, 78, 166
Hudson, A. 7
Hudson, B. 26
Huffington, C. 25, 43

identification of need 53–4
individuals, work with 76–84
Ingleby Report 21
integrated model 49–51, 174–7
inter-agency relationships 153–8

James, M. 84
Jongeward, D. 84
Jordan, B. 14, 24, 170
Joseph, Sir K. 24

Kahan, B. 25, 57, 61
KIDS Family Centre 166–7
Kirk, R. 162, 164
Kovel, J. 76

Land, H. 11
Langan, M. 6, 16
legislation 13–17
Leissner, A. 19
Leonard, D. 6, 7, 164
Liffman, M. 128, 130, 131
local authorities 19, 22, 24, 25, 27, 34, 36, 47, 154
local authority centres *see under* family centres

McCaughan, N. 91
Macdonald, S. 14, 52

McKechnie, N. 25
McMahon, L. 108
management 133–43
definitions 133–4
organisational contexts and constraints 135
power and control 135–6
staff 144–53
Manor, O. 25
Mayne, S. 41, 174
men 6, 8, 43–4, 78, 136, 146, 162–6
see also fathers
methods 49, 74–101
Miles, J. 160
Miller, C. 137
minority ethnic groups 5, 25, 47, 96, 141–2, 145, 161–2
Mittler, P. 118, 132
Monroe Young Family Centre 43
Morgan, D. 1
mothers 6–8, 16–17, 24, 43–4, 55, 89, 146, 162–5
Mumford, D. 157

National Children's Bureau 126
National Health Service and Community Care Act 15
National Institute for Social Work 137–8
need *see* identification of need; children in need
Nelson-Jones, R. 76
networks 42, 94–5, 98, 157–8, 176
nursery nursing 46, 145, 148

Oakley, A. 164
Oakley, R. 5
objectives *see* aims and objectives
Ong, B. 163
Orbach, S. 8
origins *see* family centres, origins

Packman, J. 14, 24, 170
parent advocacy *see* advocacy; parents' rights

parenting 10–11, 14, 44, 64,
115–16, 163–4, 171
groups 88
parents 42–4
inner child of 112, 114, 171
lone *see under* families
needs of 7–8, 42–4, 50–1, 167–9
partnership with *see*
partnership
responsibilities of 14
rights of 12, 13–14, 63–4
see also mothers; fathers
Parish, A. 155
Parker, R. 11, 20, 21, 22
Parsloe, P. ix, 54, 151
Parsons, T. 4
participation 23–4, 46, 51,
117–32, 175
partnership
between agencies 19, 34, 37,
153–8
with parents 23–4, 45–6, 50–1,
103, 117–32, 136, 169–70,
173–4
Parton, N. 160
Payne, C. 137, 138, 139, 151, 152
Phelan, J. 26, 31, 35, 36, 101, 123
philosophies, different 30
Pitman, E. 84
play therapy 107–8
playgroups 24, 34
Plowden Report 23, 117
Polansky, N. 50
power and control 50, 126–8,
132, 135–6
Preschool Playgroup
Association 34
Preston-Shoot, M. 91
prevention 20–2, 26–7, 30, 48, 49
Pringle, M. 21
psychotherapy 75–7
Pugh, G. 7, 104, 119, 126, 128,
132, 167, 169

Quinton, D. 10

race xiv, 7–8, 9–10, 14, 47, 58,
103, 104, 135, 145, 161–2
see also anti-racism

Race Equality Unit 5, 58
Race Relations Act 145
Rapoport, R. 2, 5
recording 61
referral 39–40, 48, 53–4
Reith, D. 57
residential care 22–3, 45
resources, provision of 68–70
role of users 45–6, 48, 171–2
see also partnership with parents
role strain 83, 171–2
Rutter, M. 10

Saunders, A. 24
Schaffer, H. 4
Scott, T. 137, 151, 152
Seebohm Report 20, 117
self-help 26
centres 33, 36–7
groups 90–1
self-referrals 39–40
service agreements 37, 154
Shaw, M. 149
Shinman, S. 25, 161
Shree Ram Krishna Centre 161
Sinclair, I. 29
Smith, T. 26, 40
Social Fund 66, 122
social policy 11–13, 27–8, 163
social services ix, 16–17, 20, 27,
34, 36, 39, 44, 64, 91, 137,
146, 154, 176
Social Services Inspectorate 31,
161
social work(ers) 27, 33, 56, 61,
68, 74, 89, 119, 145, 147, 148,
156–7
Soho Family Centre 161
Speakman, M. 6, 7, 164
Specht, H. 74
sponsoring agency 36–7, 47
staff 46–7, 144–53
and families 170–4; *see also*
partnership with parents
leadership styles 148–50
recruitment 144–6
supervision 150–3
team approach 146–8

stages of work 52–60
Statham, D. 6, 8, 163, 166
Stevenson, O. 24
Stewart, J. 134
Stewart, J.K. 46
stigma 39, 50, 92, 160, 175
Stones, C. 91
Street, E. 84
supervision *see* staff supervision

target for intervention 40–1
Taylor Report 23, 117
termination 52, 59–60
Thamesdown 26
Thomas, D. 95, 97, 143
Thorne, B. 7
Tibbenham, A. 42
transactional analysis 83–4, 171
transference 76–7
Tristam, S. 130
Trowell, J. 25, 43
Truax, C. 77
Turner, C. 13
Twelvetrees, A. 94

University Settlements 19

values 136
Vickery, A. 74

voluntary agency centres *see under*
    family centres
voluntary sector 19, 22, 26, 31,
    34, 36–7
volunteers 71–3

Walker, H. 26, 33, 44, 161, 163,
    167
Walsh, K. 153
Warnock Report 118
Warren, C. 25, 26, 33, 42, 46, 62,
    64, 74, 76, 161
welfare rights 64–8
welfare services 15–17, 27, 43, 89,
    117, 160, 161, 174–7
West Devon Family Centre 42
Williams, F. 12
Willmott, P. 41, 174
Wilson, A. 5, 8
women 4–8, 12, 15, 17, 18, 28,
    41, 43–4, 78, 89, 121, 135,
    146, 161, 162–6
    see also mothers
Wood, D. 105

Yalom, M. 7
Younghusband, E. 19